The American Occupational Therapy Association, Inc.

Educating College Students with Disabilities

What Academic & Fieldwork Educators Need to Know

The American Occupational Therapy Association, Inc.

Disclaimers

This publication is designed to provide accurate and authoritative information in regard to the subject matter covered. It is sold or distributed with the understanding that the publisher is not engaged in rendering legal, accounting, or other professional service. If legal advice or other expert assistance is required, the services of a competent professional person should be sought.

> — *From the Declaration of Principles jointly adopted by the American Bar Association and a Committee of Publishers and Associations.*

It is the objective of The American Occupational Therapy Association to be a forum for free expression and interchange of ideas. The opinions expressed by the contributors to this work are their own and not necessarily those of either the editors or the American Occupational Therapy Association.

AOTA Director of Nonperiodical Publications: Frances E. McCarrey
AOTA Managing Editor of Nonperiodical Publications: Mary C. Fisk
Designed by Teri H. Rubenstein

ISBN-1-56900-079-4

Printed in the United States of America

About the Contributors

Authors

Sally S. Scott, PhD is an Associate Director of the Learning Disabilities Center at the University of Georgia, Athens.

Shirley Wells, MPH, OT is the Manager of the Multicultural Affairs Program at the American Occupational Therapy Association National Office, Bethesda, Maryland.

Sandy Hanebrink, OTS is an occupational therapy student at the Medical University of South Carolina, Charleston.

Contributor

Kimberly Hartmann, MHS, OTR/L, FAOTA is the Occupational Therapy Program Director at Quinnipiac College, Hamden, Connecticut.

Preface
· ·

Several years ago, when I was the Assistant Dean of the School of Occupational Therapy at Texas Woman's University, Dallas Campus, a young woman with cerebral palsy registered for senior-level courses in our baccalaureate program. She had successfully completed all coursework at the Denton campus and had a high grade point average, but coursework in Dallas differed from lower-division coursework. This would be a year of learning occupational therapy assessments and interventions, including physical disabilities and pediatrics labs, which required handling techniques, transfer skills, and splint fabrication. The student used an electric wheelchair, had severe impairment of fine motor skills, and a marked speech impediment. Yet, in spite of her physical limitations, she functioned quite independently, drove her own car, and managed a household as the single parent of a well-groomed 6-year-old.

During the first week of the semester, the faculty gathered to discuss this student and established consensus that according to the requirements of TWU's Office of Special Student Services and ADA regulations, it was incumbent upon the student to complete the necessary paperwork to declare her disability and request accommodation for each course in which she enrolled. But faculty had many questions about how far they were expected to go in order to accommodate this student. In a course that included learning and performing various transfer techniques, should this requirement be waived? The pediatrics instructor wondered how the student could demonstrate handling techniques in the neurodevelopmental treatment lab. The physical disabilities instructor recognized that the student would not be able to place and move a goniometer to take accurate joint measurements. Splint fabrication was out of the question.

Because ADA was a relatively recent law, few of us had experience with essential functions of an occupational therapy student and we were in a quandary about reasonable accommodations. In search of advice, I contacted the American Occupational Therapy Association, only to learn that there were no easy answers, no instant solutions, but that the issue was being addressed by the Commission on Education and the Education Program Directors. In fact, I learned that one of the program directors, Kim Hartmann, was drafting a proposal for a publication on the topic of accommodation for occupational therapy students with disabilities.

You can imagine how delighted I am to see this book completed. In my position as Education Director at AOTA I am well aware of the increase in the number of technical- and professional-level students with disabilities. The calls received at the National Office regarding students with disabilities have increased remarkably, especially those calls regarding fieldwork issues. In the 1995 *Education Data Survey*, 3% of professional-level students, a total of 390 students, identified themselves as "disabled" or as having disabling conditions. Of those students, the most common conditions were learning disabilities (17.9%), orthopedic disabilities (10.5%), chronic medical conditions (9.5%), and emotional problems (8.5%). In technical-level programs 418 students identified themselves as "disabled" or as having a disabling conditions. Learning disabilities again topped the list for those OTA students (30%), as well as orthopedic disabilities (16%), emotional problems (11%), and chronic medical conditions (9%). These figures represent a continuous rise in students with disabilities between 1988 and 1994.[1] For an updated report the most recent *Education Data Survey* will be available in the fall of 1997 from AOTA.

This book brings together a wealth of information to assist OT and OTA educators with challenging issues regarding students with disabilities while allaying fears of lawsuits. Readers need to realize that the trend in court decisions in higher education programs is usually to uphold the academic institution and the standards of the profession. Academic faculty and fieldwork educators alike will find this book a useful tool in clarifying the rights of students with disabilities as well as the right of the profession to uphold its standards.

My hope is that this book will be both a resource and a stimulus for thought. All of us in this profession must determine the essential functions required to be an occupational therapy practitioner. Obviously, the critical thinking skills used to plan programs that will enable our clients to lead more functional lives are an essential function. Must every practitioner also be expected to provide the hands on techniques to achieve these goals?

— *Rhona Zukas, MOT, OTR, FAOTA*
Director, AOTA Education Department

---

[1] American Occupational Therapy Association. *Education Data Survey Final Report.* 1995.

Table of Contents

Chapter 1—Legal Foundations *by Sally S. Scott* 1
  Overview of Federal Law 1
  Terminology 2
  Implementing Regulations 2
    Admission and Recruitment 3
    Treatment of Students (General) 3
    Academic Adjustments 4
    Housing 5
    Financial and Employment Assistance 5
    Nonacademic Services 5
  Student and Faculty Rights and Responsibilities 5
  Summary 7
  References 8
  Recommended Readings 8

Chapter 2—Investigating Existing Institutional Resources and Establishing Linkages *by Sally S. Scott* 9
  Existing Structures 9
    Required Campus Access Services 9
    Campus Support Structures 9
    Typical Functions of a Campus Office for Students with Disabilities 10
    Campuses Without an Office for Students with Disabilities 11
  Campus Resources 11
    The Office for Students with Disabilities 12
    ADA/Section 504 Compliance Officer 12
    OT Students with Disabilities 12
    Campuswide Disability Advisory Board 13
    Student Advocacy Groups or Student Bureaus 13
    Faculty with Relevant Expertise 13
  Summary 13
  References 13
  Recommended Readings 13

Chapter 3—Technical Standards and Essential Requirements *by Shirley Wells and Sandy Hanebrink with contributions from Kimberly Hartmann* 15
  Qualified Students 15
  Technical Standards 17
  Determining Technical Standards 18
  Samples of Technical Standards and Essential Program Requirements 19
    Program Minimum Skills for Eligibility to Participate in Educational Programs and Activities 19
    University of Minnesota Programs in Occupational and Physical Therapy: Clinical/Fieldwork Environment Checklist 20
    University of Minnesota Occupational Therapy Student Performance Essentials and Critical Demands (4/15/93) 21
    Didactic Preparation 21
      Clinical Fieldwork Experience 22
    Lourdes College OTA Program 23
      Essential Functions of a COTA and Candidate/Student for the Lourdes College OTA Program 23
  Essential Program Requirements 25
    Establishing Essential Program Requirements 26
    Identifying the Essential Functions of the Program 26

Determining Essential Components 26
Writing Essential Program Requirements 28
Determining Clinical and Fieldwork Requirements 29
Samples of Essential Program Requirements 29
 Texas Woman's University
 Denton/Dallas/Houston, Texas 29
General Outline for Essential Elements for Occupational Therapy
College of St. Scholastica
Duluth, Minnesota
Occupational Therapy Department
Contract of Professional Behaviors 31
 Professor Responsibilities and Student Rights 31
 Student Responsibilities With or Without Reasonable Accommodations 32
Lasell College
Occupational Therapy Assistant Program 33
 Essential Functions 33
Documentation 33
Dissemination 34
Summary 34
References 35

Chapter 4—Auxiliary Aids, Academic Adjustments, and Reasonable Accommodations
 by Shirley Wells and Sandy Hanebrink with contributions from Kimberly Hartmann 37
Defining Reasonable Accommodation 37
Academic Adjustment 39
 Test-Taking Accommodations 39
 Waiving a Course/Examination Requirement 41
 Tape Recorders 41
 Auxiliary Aids and Services 41
 Honoring Communication Choice 41
 Fee for Services 41
 Interpreter Services 42
 Real-Time Stenocaptioning 42
 Notetakers 42
 Readers 43
 Alternative Formats 43
 Computer Equipment 43
 Personal Services 44
 Dissatisfaction with Accommodations 44
Contractual Agreements/Field Placement 44
Academic Accommodation Process 46
Summary 49
References 49

Chapter 5—Procedural Considerations *by Sally S. Scott* 53
Dissemination and Use of OT Standards and Policies 53
 Dissemination of Standards and Policies 53
 Student Outreach 54
 Faculty Outreach 54
 Use of Standards and Policies 55
Recruitment and Admission 55
 General OT Student Treatment 57
Working with Individual Students 57
 Students Who Self-Identify 57
 Students with Suspected Disabilities 58
 Processing Accommodation Requests 59
 Student Responsibilities 59

Faculty Responsibilities 60
Denial of Accommodations 61
    Legitimate Objections 64
Coordinating Efforts Between the OT Department and the Clinical Site 65
    Promoting Clinical Site Accessibility 65
Working with Students Across Sites: Frequent Questions 65
References 67

Chapter 6—Student Empowerment *by Sally S. Scott* **69**
Individual Faculty Strategies 69
    Reflecting on Personal Attitudes 69
    Advocating for Adequate Institutional Policies and Structures 70
    Encouraging Student Self-Identification 70
    Terminology 72
    General Etiquette 73
    Support Transitions 74
        Secondary to Postsecondary 74
Successful Adults with Learning Disabilities 75
    Factors in Success 75
    Implications for OT Faculty 76
Summary 77
References 77
Recommended Readings 78

Chapter 7—Resources **79**
On-Campus Resources 79
Local Resources—State 79
Regional Resources—Office of Civil Rights (OCR) 79
    Government Offices—Section 504 79
    Office of Civil Rights 80
    Regional Disability and Business Technical Assistance Centers (DBTACs)—Contact for
    Information on the ADA 82
    Other Government Resources 83
    National Resources 83
    Publications 87
    Technology 88

Index **91**

The key to compliance with disability discrimination laws is balancing the rights of disabled individuals with the institution's desire to preserve the integrity of its programs.

— S. Heyward, 1992

Legal Foundations

Sally S. Scott

On July 29, 1990, President George Bush signed into law the Americans with Disabilities Act (ADA) and ensured equal rights to over 49 million individuals with disabilities. The ADA is a significant and wide-reaching piece of civil rights legislation that prohibits colleges and universities, as well as other public and private entities, from discriminating against individuals with disabilities. Section 504 of the Rehabilitation Act of 1973 was a precursor to the ADA and served to establish many of the requirements and procedures for institutions of higher education in providing an equal educational opportunity for individuals with disabilities. Both federal mandates stipulate that individuals with disabilities must be provided equal opportunities for admission to colleges and, if admitted, equivalent access to the educational experience. This chapter provides an overview of these federal laws, examines relevant terminology, reviews the implementing regulations—including specific implications for occupational therapy (OT) faculty and outlines the resulting rights and responsibilities of students with disabilities and OT faculty.

Overview of Federal Law

Section 504 of the Rehabilitation Act of 1973 (29 USCA Sec. 794) states, "No otherwise qualified individual with disabilities in the United States shall solely by reason of his/her disability be excluded from participation in, be denied the benefits of, or be subjected to discrimination under any program or activity receiving federal financial assistance." The wording of the law is broad in order to be applicable to a wide range of college settings and individual contexts, but the intent of the law is clear—individuals with disabilities are to be provided equal access to higher education. Equal access pertains to both physical and programmatic considerations. However, institutions of higher education are not required to lower standards or to create special programs (Heyward, 1992). Federal financial assistance has been clarified as including student financial aid (*Grove City College v. Bell*, 1984), and receipt of federal monies by any department within a postsecondary institution triggers the accountability of the entire institution under Section 504 (Civil Rights Restoration Act of 1987). Hence, few institutions of higher education are exempt from the mandates of Section 504.

The ADA is based on the same principles and beliefs as Section 504 and, in fact, draws upon much of its terminology. However, the ADA extends the nondiscrimination mandate beyond merely federal financial recipients and applies to a wide range of public and private establishments. Five distinct titles within the law delineate requirements for nondiscrimination across a broad spectrum of society including employment (Title I); state and local government, including public institutions of higher education (Title II, Subpart A), as well as transportation (Title II, Subpart B); public accommodations, including independent colleges (Title III); telecommunications (Title IV); and miscellaneous provisions (Title V).

In most instances, if a postsecondary institution is in compliance with Section 504, it will be nondiscriminatory under the ADA as well. However, where ADA standards are more stringent and provide greater protection for individuals with disabilities, institutions of higher education must comply with the ADA (Jarrow, 1992b; Kincaid & Simon, 1994). Though few new requirements are mandated of institutions of higher education, the ADA's extension of nondiscrimination mandates to public and private licensure or certification programs and to the employment sector is of significance to college faculty. It provides the assurance that accommodations and academic adjustments required in college programs will also be available to individuals with disabilities in licensing and certification exams (Title II, Sec. 35.130 and Title III, Sec. 36.309) and after college graduation in the employment sector. These access requirements serve to assuage concerns that college services and accommodations are not preparing individuals with disabilities for employment in the "real world."

Terminology

Both Section 504 and the ADA contain several key terms warranting definition. An *individual with a disability* is someone who has a physical or mental impairment that substantially limits a major life activity, has a record or history of such an impairment or is regarded as having such an impairment (Section 504, Subpart A). Major life activities include walking, seeing, hearing, speaking, breathing, learning, working, caring for oneself, and performing manual tasks. Typical kinds of disabilities include learning disabilities, physical disabilities, sensory impairments, psychological disabilities, traumatic brain injuries, alcohol or drug addiction (excluding current illegal drug use), attention deficit disorders, and so forth.

Institutions of higher education are required to provide admission only to those individuals with disabilities who are otherwise qualified. An *otherwise qualified* individual with a disability is one who can meet the academic and technical standards for admission to the institution or program with or without accommodation. *Technical standards* refer to all nonacademic criteria used for admission to and participation in a program. These may include physical requirements if they are essential to the

program and applied equally to all applicants (*Davis v. Southeastern Community College*, 1979).

Colleges are not required to compromise or lower essential requirements of a course or program. Essential requirements may be established by the college. However, the essential standards must be legitimate, rationally related to the goals and objectives of the program, and applied in a nondiscriminatory way (*Doe v. New York University*, 1981; *Pushkin v. Regents of the University of Colorado*, 1981; *Wynne v. Tufts University School of Medicine*, 1992). The process of defining essential functions within an OT training program will be discussed in chapter 3.

Institutions must provide reasonable accommodations to college applicants and, if admitted, in general student treatment. A reasonable accommodation is not a standard formula but rather entails a reasoning process in which essential requirements of the course or program, individual student abilities, and possible accommodations are considered. *Reasonable accommodations* may be relatively straightforward such as scheduling classes in accessible buildings or providing a sign language interpreter. They may also become more complex in such situations as providing alternative means of evaluating student academic achievement or substituting specific courses required for the completion of degree requirements. The process of determining a reasonable accommodation in an OT academic or clinical setting will be discussed in detail in chapter 4.

Implementing Regulations

In addition to federal law providing broad principles of nondiscrimination, implementing regulations for Section 504 were established in 1978. Subpart E of the regulations pertains specifically to the context of postsecondary education. The regulations provide more specific guidance within various arenas of higher education and clarify that virtually all aspects of postsecondary education must be made accessible to individuals with disabilities (see Table 1.1). To provide perspective on the range and scope of institutional responsibility to individuals with disabilities, each area of the implementing regulations will be summarized. Areas with specific implications for OT classroom and clinical faculty will be discussed in more detail.

Table 1.1
Areas Within Higher Education That Must be Accessible

- Admission and recruitment

- Treatment of students (general)

- Academic adjustments (including academic requirements, course examinations, and auxiliary aids)

- Housing

- Financial and employment assistance

- Nonacademic services

Admission and Recruitment

Equal access in the areas of *admission and recruitment* (Section 104.42) means that students with disabilities may not be excluded from recruitment activities and that qualified students with disabilities may not be denied admission on the basis of disability. Nondiscrimination is not a mandate for affirmative action efforts by the institution. Rather, the institution is required to make admission decisions based on the student's ability to meet the academic and technical standards of the institution with or without reasonable accommodation. Typical accommodations in the admissions process include taking standardized college entrance exams such as the Scholastic Achievement Test (SAT) or the American College Testing (ACT) Program with accommodation (e.g., use of a scribe or large print) and providing additional information such as a personal essay or interview to describe compensation strategies and learning strengths that may not be conveyed in traditional admission criteria. Of

significance to OT classroom and clinical faculty, admission standards are not lowered for students with disabilities. Students who have been admitted to the institution have met admission criteria in spite of their disabilities and have been deemed "otherwise qualified."

Treatment of Students (General)

Equal access in *treatment of students (general)* (Section 104.43) means that, once admitted, the student with a disability is to be a full and active participant in the full range of programs and activities of the institution. The institution is prohibited from discriminating under any academic, research, occupational training, health insurance, counseling, transportation, or extracurricular activity. One area in which this regulation will impact OT faculty is in the admission of students with disabilities into the OT program itself. Students with disabilities may not be excluded from the program simply because of the presence of a disability or because of an assumption that they will not be able to find employment in the field. Students with disabilities must, however, meet the same criteria required of all other students for admission to the OT program. For example, if a grade point average of 3.2 is required to enter the OT program, this standard may be held for students with disabilities as well. Students with disabilities should, of course, have been provided reasonable accommodations in the coursework contributing to the grade point average (GPA). If a minimum grade is required within a specific prerequisite course, if completion of prerequisite courses is required within a specified time limit, or if a specific number of hours observing and volunteering in OT environments is required of all applicants, then these same criteria may be applied to students with disabilities as well. If specific technical standards such as sensation in the hands, ability to communicate directly through speech or sign, or ability to interpret environmental and client information regarding safety are required of all students in order to successfully participate in the OT program, students with disabilities must meet these technical standards as well. It is not considered discriminatory to deny students with disabilities admission to a program of study if they do not meet academic and technical admission standards. These standards must, however, be logically related to the program and applied to all applicants in a nondiscriminatory fashion. (See chapter 5 for a discussion of important principles in weighing admissions decisions.)

Another area of general student treatment that will impact OT classroom and clinical faculty is the required accessibility of clinical training sites. OT training programs typically consider both academic and clinical components to be essential in preparing OT professionals. The courts have upheld this as a logical essential requirement in similar training programs such as nursing (*Davis v. Southeastern Community College*, 1979). If both components of training are considered essential and required of all OT students, then the OT faculty must ensure that clinical training is also accessible to students with disabilities under the same nondiscrimination standards as every other program at the institution even if the college does not directly operate the clinical site (34 CFR, Subpart E, Section 104.43[b]). If one clinical site is used by all students, then that site must be accessible for students with disabilities. If a range of clinical sites are used by various students in the program, this does not mean that all clinical sites must be fully accessible. The law requires that, when viewed in its entirety, the OT program offers students with disabilities the same range and quality of choice in clinical sites as are available to other students in the program. For example, all OT students who are wheelchair users may not be required to study at one clinical site if other OT students have the option to select clinical sites that offer opportunities for using more high-tech equipment or for studying with specialized or renowned professionals within the field of OT. Students with disabilities must be given the same range of options for benefiting from the OT classroom and clinical program.

Academic Adjustments

Equal access in *academic adjustments* (Section 104.44) includes the specific areas of academic requirements (104.44[a]), course examinations (104.44[c]), and auxiliary aids (104.44[d]). This regulation has direct impact on OT faculty in both the classroom and clinical settings. It stipulates that the institution (including OT faculty) must consider reasonable accommodations that do not compromise essential academic requirements of a course or program. Based on individual student need and specific requirements, this may include modification in length of time permitted for completion of degree requirements, substitution of specific courses, or adaptation of the manner in which courses are conducted. The institution must ensure that course evaluations represent student achievement in the course rather than the student's disability. This may include such accommodations as providing extended time, testing in a distraction-free environment, or testing in an alternate format (e.g., essay instead of multiple choice, oral instead of written). The institution must also ensure that students with disabilities are not discriminated against because of the absence of auxiliary aids. Auxiliary aids include such services and actions as taped texts, interpreters, readers, note takers, and so forth, though services of a personal nature need not be provided. This regulation captures the essence of nondiscriminatory faculty–student interaction in the teaching and learning process. It also constitutes the primary area needing attention by OT faculty in ensuring a nondiscriminatory OT training program. Addressing each aspect of this regulation while maintaining program and institutional integrity will receive detailed attention in the subsequent sections of this book, including defining essential requirements (chapter 3), weighing reasonable accommodations (chapter 4), and considering issues in implementation (chapter 5).

Housing

Equal access to *housing* (Section 104.45) means that the institution must provide comparable, convenient, and accessible housing for students with disabilities.

Financial and Employment Assistance

Equal access to *financial and employment assistance* (Section 104.46) means that colleges may not limit eligibility or provide less assistance to qualified students with disabilities. Though not likely to influence the activities of OT faculty specifically, these areas of nondiscrimination play an important role in providing access to college and in the subsequent satisfaction and retention of OT students with disabilities.

Nonacademic Services

Equal access to and reasonable accommodation of *nonacademic services* (Section 104.47) means that students with disabilities must be provided comparable opportunities and services in the areas of physical education and athletics, counseling and placement services, and social organizations. Of specific relevance to OT faculty is the area of academic counseling. OT faculty may not counsel students with disabilities out of the OT field or toward more restrictive career objectives based on stereotypes of the disability label. For example, it would be discriminatory for an OT faculty member to advise a student that individuals with learning disabilities should not consider the OT profession. It is permissible, however, for faculty to discuss specific strengths and weaknesses in relevant performance areas including factual information about licensing and certification requirements that may present obstacles based on the individual student's actual performance in the program.

Student and Faculty Rights and Responsibilities

In addition to the broad requirements of federal law and the implementing regulations, case law has helped to further clarify some rights and responsibilities of both students with disabilities and faculty in ensuring equal access to higher education. As seen in Table 1.2, student and faculty rights are largely established in the implementing regulations (discussed in the previous section) and have been reinforced through case law. Student and faculty responsibilities, however, entail enacting these nondiscriminatory principles, and case law has clarified procedural roles in requesting and attaining reasonable accommodations. An overview of emergent rights and responsibilities for students with disabilities and OT faculty drawn from each of these sources will be discussed briefly.

Students with disabilities have the right to access the full college experience, including the opportunity to learn and be evaluated based on individual abilities rather than disabilities (Sections 104.43, 104.44). In order to receive accommodation, however, the student with a disability must first self-identify as having a disability and request accommodation (*Salvador v. Bell*, 1985). The institution has no responsibility to accommodate the student until the individual initiates this process. Similarly, OT classroom and clinical faculty who have not been notified of a student's disability or who have not been requested to accommodate a student have no obligation to anticipate a student's disability-related needs. Indeed, some students with disabilities will intentionally elect not to utilize accommodations and faculty need to be aware of and respect this right. The mandate for accommodation is not retroactive, and faculty responsibility only begins at the point of notification and request for accommodation (*Salvador v. Bell*, 1985).

Table 1.2
Rights and Responsibilities of Students with
Disabilities and Occupational Therapy Faculty

STUDENTS WITH DISABILITIES

Rights

- To be provided meaningful access to the full range of programs and activities of the institution

- To receive an equal educational opportunity for learning

- To be evaluated based on abilities rather than disabilities

Responsibilities (If accommodation is requested)

- To self-identify as having a disability

- To provide documentation of the disability

- To request accommodation

- To follow institutional policies and procedures

- To monitor the effectiveness of the accommodation

- To meet the academic and technical standards required of all students

OCCUPATIONAL THERAPY FACULTY

Rights

- To maintain course and program integrity

- To preserve academic freedom

Responsibilities

- To define essential course, clinical, and program components

- To provide/permit reasonable accommodations based on individual student need

- To permit the use of necessary auxiliary aids

- To evaluate students based on abilities rather than disabilities

- To use accessible on- and off-campus sites and provide a comparable range of opportunities in training and learning experiences

If required by the institution, the student must provide acceptable documentation of the disability. This may be particularly relevant with students with "invisible" disabilities such as learning disabilities or attention deficit disorders. It is not the responsibility of the institution to conduct evaluations to document the existence of a disability. Diagnostic information is considered medical documentation and, as such, must be kept confidential by the campus office for students with disabilities (Jarrow, 1992a). The student with a disability should be encouraged to discuss learning strengths and needs with individual OT faculty (see chapter 6 for strategies for student empowerment in this process) or, with a signed release from the student, personnel from the campus disability support office may discuss individual student needs with faculty. The faculty member, however, does not have the right to access individual student disability documentation (Jarrow, 1992a).

The institution and individual faculty must provide students with reasonable accommodations, but the student must follow any institutional procedures for requesting accommodation (Heyward, Lawton, & Associates, 1992). Students must also monitor the effectiveness of the accommodation and request adjustments or alternate accommodations as needed. The student must continue to meet the academic and technical standards required of all other students at the institution (*Anderson v. University of Wisconsin*, 1988; *McGregor v. Louisiana State University*, 1992). For students in an OT program, this may entail successful performance in both classroom and clinical components of the program if these have been defined as essential for all students in the program (*Doherty v. Southern College of Optometry*, 1988).

In turn, faculty have specific rights and responsibilities in the process of accommodation and access for students with disabilities. Faculty have the right to maintain course and program integrity primarily through the process of defining essential course and program components that must be

achieved by all students (*Heyward, 1992; Wynne v. Tufts University School of Medicine*, 1992). In clinical training sites this right extends to defining essential functions and activities that students must be able to perform in the clinical setting. Faculty have the right to academic freedom in their individual classrooms, yet this right does not supersede the civil rights of students with disabilities for nondiscrimination (*Dinsmore v. Pugh and the Regents of the University of California at Berkeley*, settled 1989, cited in Heyward, Lawton, & Associates, 1991) nor does this right necessarily conflict with the student's civil rights (Scott, 1994).

Classroom and clinical faculty must permit the use of auxiliary aids necessary for student access including, for example, allowing the use of a tape recorder in the classroom or allowing a guide dog to be brought into the clinical site (Section 104.44[d]). The faculty member has the responsibility to evaluate students based on their abilities, including use of alternate test formats that do not compromise essential requirements (Section 104.44[c]). And finally, the faculty member has the responsibility to use accessible sites for on- and off-campus learning and training to ensure that students with disabilities have access to a comparable range of classroom and clinical experiences (Section 104.43).

Summary

In this chapter, we have provided a brief overview of the legal foundations for equal opportunity for individuals with disabilities and program integrity for institutions of higher education. From this foundation, the remainder of the book will focus on how to implement procedures that preserve program integrity and protect the rights of college students with disabilities in OT training programs.

● ● ●

References

Americans with Disabilities Act, 1990, P.L. 101-336, 42 U.S.C. Sec. 12101.

Anderson v. University of Wisconsin, 841 F. 2D 737 (7th Cir.) 1988.

Civil Rights Restoration Act of 1987, P.L. 100-259, 29 U.S.C. Sec. 794(a)(2)(A).

Davis v. Southeastern Community College, 442 U.S. 397, 99S. Ct. 2361, 6OL. Ed. 2D 980, 1979.

Dinsmore v. Pugh and the Regents of the University of California at Berkeley, (settled) 1989. Heyward, Lawton, & Associates (1991). Provision of academic accommodations. *Disability Accommodation Digest, 1* (1), 1, 4. 50 U.S.L.W. 2366.

Doe v. New York University, 50 U.S.L.W. 2366 (2nd Cir.) 1981.

Doherty v. Southern College of Optometry, 862 F. 2D 570 (6th Cir.) 1988.

Grove City College v. Bell, 465 U.S. 555, 104S. Ct. 1211, 79L. Ed. 2D 516, 1984.

Heyward, S. (1992). *Access to education for the disabled: A guide to compliance with Section 504 of the Rehabilitation Act of 1973.* Jefferson, NC: McFarland & Company.

Heyward, S., Lawton, & Associates. (1992). Developing a compliance program that works. *Disability Accommodation Digest, 2,* 4.

Jarrow, J. (1992a). *Subpart E: The impact of Section 504 on postsecondary education.* Columbus, OH: AHEAD.

Jarrow, J. (1992b). *Title by title: The ADA's impact on postsecondary education.* Columbus, OH: AHEAD.

Kincaid, J., & Simon J. (1994). *Issues in higher education and disability law.* Columbus, OH: AHEAD.

McGregor v. Louisiana State University, Board of Supervisors, Civ. No. 91-4328 (E.D. La.) 1992.

Pushkin v. Regents of the University of Colorado, 685 F. 2D 1372 (10th Cir.) 1981.

Rehabilitation Act of 1973, Section 504, P.L. 93-112, 29 U.S.C. Sec. 794 (1977).

Salvador v. Bell, 622 F. Supp. 438 (N.D. Ill.) 1985.

Scott, S. (1994). Determining reasonable academic adjustments for college students with learning disabilities. *Journal of Learning Disabilities, 27,* 403–412.

Wynne v. Tufts University School of Medicine, 976 F. 2D 791 (1st Cir.) 1992.

Recommended Readings

Essex-Sorlie, D. (July, 1994). The Americans with Disabilities Act: Implications and suggestions for compliance for medical schools. *Academic Medicine,* 525–527.

Rothstein, L. (1991). Students, staff, and faculty with disabilities: Current issues for colleges and universities. *Journal of College and University Law, 17*(4), 471–482.

CHAPTER 2

Only by collaborating and pooling talent and resources can you come up with the best ideas and the best mechanisms to solve shared problems.

— R. Jacobsen, (Melaville, Blank, & Aseyesh, 1993)

Investigating Existing Institutional Resources and Establishing Linkages

Sally S. Scott

The first step in establishing procedures for a non-discriminatory OT program is to realize that there are a number of existing services, structures, and resources both on- and off-campus that can assist in this process. In this chapter, we focus on important institutional resources and supports, and the linkages with these structures that are essential to the successful development and implementation of OT policies pertaining to students with disabilities. We also suggest potential campus resources to provide ongoing assistance in the process of promoting the accessibility of the OT program.

Existing Structures

Because the federal mandate for college access has been in place since 1973 and applies to programs, services, and activities campuswide, there will likely be contact people, structures, and/or resources already in place on campus to address some of the needs of students with disabilities. Within this mandate for college access, however, neither the law nor the implementing regulations specify exactly how colleges should structure or provide services. As a result, campus supports vary widely. In this chapter, we provide a brief review of what services colleges are required to provide, an overview of different structures that have resulted from broad federal mandates, and a description of typical functions of campus support offices (typically referred to as the Office for Students with Disabilities, or OSD).

Required Campus Access Services

The implementing regulations of Section 504 stipulate that college campuses are required to provide: (1) initial and continuing steps to notify individuals with disabilities that the institution does not discriminate on the basis of disability (Subpart A, Section 104.8[a]); (2) a campus contact person to coordinate efforts to comply with federal law (Section 104.7[a]); (3) continuing efforts to disseminate the name and contact information of the campus coordinator (Section 104.8[a]); and (4) grievance procedures for the resolution of complaints about discriminatory actions (Section 104.7[b]). Case law has further clarified that postsecondary institutions must have established procedures for students with disabilities to access accommodations, address issues, and resolve conflicts pertaining to equal access (*Brown v. Washington University*, 1990).

Campus Support Structures

Despite the common mandate for disability access, postsecondary institutions have responded with support services and mechanisms that are quite diverse.

By nature, colleges across the country vary widely according to their mission, faculty and staff, student body, course offerings, financial resources, size, location, and so forth. Similarly, access to these diverse campuses also varies widely to meet local needs, purposes, and priorities.

Often the philosophy of the support office and the resulting services will be in keeping with the general mission of the institution. For example, a community college with strong commitment to meeting the needs of a diverse student population through instruction and programming will be more likely to offer remedial coursework and services for its students with disabilities as well. A small 4-year liberal arts institution that prides itself on teaching excellence and a nurturing environment might provide students with disabilities more opportunities for interaction with faculty and emphasize instruction and counseling more closely catered to individual needs. And finally, large institutions focusing on research and scholarship may offer a broader range of supports but serve large numbers of students in less individualized or personal ways.

Within general campus philosophies, however, colleges are responding to ubiquitous mandates for access at different rates and with different levels of commitment. Scott (1996) has provided an overview of the range of college support services that currently exist on college campuses. Supports are characterized along a continuum ranging from decentralized and limited services (Level 1) to comprehensive services (Level 4). Campus supports range from no formal contact person for disability issues to multiple staff with various areas of disability expertise; a limited range of accommodations provided for students with disabilities to a full range of accommodation options; no formal institutional policies to comprehensive access and grievance procedures. Regardless of where your institution falls on the continuum of disability support structures, it is important to identify campus structures and coordinate access efforts. OT faculty wishing to identify existing institutional structures may wish to investigate the following questions: (1) Who is the campus contact person for ADA/504 compliance? (2) Who is the campus contact person for coordinating accommodation requests? (3) What accommodations are frequently provided on your campus? (4) What policies exist pertaining to disability access? and (5) Are there other campus supports such as peer support groups, special course offerings, transition services, faculty training opportunities, or a campus disability advisory board? Each of these existing institutional supports may provide a different perspective on access needs, serve as a helpful support to emerging efforts in the OT program, or provide a resource to which faculty may refer OT students with disabilities.

Typical Functions of a Campus Office for Students with Disabilities

This "office" is sometimes just a designated individual who also serves other functions at the institution. Alternatively, the office may be a highly specialized support structure with multiple staff. Whatever size or shape at an institution, the OSD typically serves as the coordination point on campus for efforts to provide accommodations and access for students with disabilities. Though the activities and procedures of support offices may vary somewhat on different campuses, there are some typical support functions that OT faculty should be aware of in order to access services, make appropriate student referrals, and coordinate or communicate OT-specific procedures.

OSDs are the location where students with disabilities register for services and request accommodation at the college. To register for services, students typically must self-identify as having a disability to the office service provider and provide any needed documentation of disability-related access needs. A campus may or may not provide diagnostic testing for students who need further documentation. Though not a requirement by federal law, some colleges have elected to provide this service. Documentation is kept confidential at the support office. The service provider at the disability support office typically has knowledge of disability documentation and physical and programmatic access issues. The service provider can review the documentation (preferably with the student), determine its adequacy, and provide recommendations for general accommodations the student may need. Often the service provider will develop a letter outlining individual student accommodation needs that the student may then deliver to specific faculty members. In this way, colleges have a centralized office for processing individual student needs, have a "quality control" mechanism for screening accommodation requests, can protect the confidentiality of students with disabilities, and are better able to monitor campus efforts and activities to meet nondiscrimination mandates. The service provider in the OSD often serves the dual role of student advocate in helping students to understand and negotiate institutional procedures and institutional guardian in ensuring that the integrity and rights of the faculty and college are protected.

As OT faculty begin to scrutinize their practices with students with disabilities, it is important to investigate the specific procedures on a campus (if not already known) to ensure that all OT students with disabilities are referred through existing institutional channels. OT faculty may legitimately refuse to accommodate a student with a disability until he or she has followed institutional procedures for registering with the institution's support office (Heyward, Lawton, & Associates, 1995). By requiring all OT students with disabilities to follow institutional channels, one will tap a resource designed to assist in protecting the integrity of the institution and allow students to benefit from the expertise of the designated campus resource on recommending potential accommodation requests.

Campuses Without an Office for Students with Disabilities

The number of campuses with disability support offices is steadily increasing. If, however, in an investigation of existing campus supports, one finds that an institution is one of the relatively small number of campuses that does not have an OSD, a disability contact person, or an adequate mechanism for collecting disability documentation and processing student accommodation requests, we encourage the individual to advocate with the administration for such services on campus. They are essential to ensuring nondiscriminatory practices for students with disabilities campuswide and provide a valuable means for protecting the integrity of the institution while meeting federal mandates. An OSD often provides a number of other valuable services to students with disabilities and to faculty. These additional supports and other campus resources present possible linkages that can assist OT faculty in developing nondiscriminatory practices.

Campus Resources

Though OT faculty are experts in their chosen field, they may have little or no training or experience in working with college students with disabilities or with negotiating the legal mandates that are very specific to the context of higher education. Federal law does not require OT faculty to become college disability experts. It does, however, require that OT faculty not discriminate against individuals with disabilities. Certain aspects of nondiscrimination in OT programs can only be defined by OT faculty themselves, as we will discuss in depth in chapters 3 and 4. However, as part of an academic community, OT faculty will better serve students with disabilities by communicating and collaborating with other campus resources. A number of campus resources on disability issues may already exist (see Table 2.1). Many of these resources are not mandated by law, but have likely evolved from the local interests and needs on campus. We encourage consideration of these various perspectives and the support and feedback they may be able to provide in faculty endeavors to develop an accessible OT program.

The Office for Students with Disabilities

The *Office for Students with Disabilities* can be a valuable resource to OT clinical and classroom faculty in their daily interactions with students as well as in the development and review of OT policies and practices. The service provider may (with the student's signed permission) provide faculty with consultation about individual student situations, including, for example, recommended accommodation strategies, suggested instructional approaches, or additional supports. Service providers may be a valuable source of information specific to college access issues. They often keep up with the rapidly emerging legal guidance on requirements for access on college campuses. They may have a library of relevant and specialized literature that would be of assistance to OT faculty. Service providers also frequently provide or coordinate faculty development efforts pertaining to student disability needs and may be available to work directly with OT faculty on requested topics.

In addition to faculty resources, the disability services office may also provide numerous services to students with disabilities such as individual case management, study skills instruction, or self-advocacy stu-

dents with disabilities such as individual case management, study skills instruction, or self-advocacy skills development. OT students with disabilities may benefit from these services and be better able to perform in and benefit from the OT training opportunities. Given their direct involvement on a daily basis with access issues, the OSD would likely be a valuable support in developing and/or reviewing OT policies and practices. (This process is discussed in more detail in chapters 3 and 4.)

ADA/Section 504 Compliance Officer

The *ADA/504 compliance officer* is typically the individual on campus charged with ensuring the institution's adherence to federal law. This individual may or may not be housed in the OSD and often is not the individual responsible for providing support services for students with disabilities. The ADA/504 compliance officer may be a valuable resource on legal requirements and current campus efforts to meet these requirements, and as such may be important to involve in the development or review of OT essential standards. (Again, this is discussed in chapters 3 and 4 in more detail.)

OT Students with Disabilities

An extremely valuable resource to OT faculty in reviewing the current accessibility of the classroom and clinical components of the OT program as well as evolving policies and practices will be *OT students with disabilities* themselves. Student feedback can be gathered in a number of ways including formalized surveys or informal interviews depending on numbers and individual needs. Students with disabilities should be involved in the development of OT procedures as well as in the ongoing review of policy effectiveness. As with all students, some students with disabilities will be more vocal and better self-advocates than others. It is important, however, to include the perspectives of individuals with disabilities in the process of defining policies and practices.

Campuswide Disability Advisory Board

Many campuses are finding it beneficial to develop a *campuswide disability advisory board*. These structures vary somewhat in their membership and activities, but often they consist of a cross-section of campus membership including administrators, faculty, students with disabilities, staff from the OSD, and representatives from community agencies such as vocational rehabilitation. Some advisory boards focus on legal compliance issues on campus while others take a broader perspective and monitor the needs and issues of students with disabilities. Depending on the focus of the advisory board, this may be an appropriate group to review and provide feedback on OT policies or may be a relevant body to which to refer OT students with disabilities when access issues arise.

Student Advocacy Groups or Student Bureaus

On some campuses, students with disabilities have organized *student advocacy groups or speakers bureaus*. These groups are typically made up of current college students with disabilities who are willing to talk about their experiences in making the transition to and adjusting to a college setting. A meeting with these students may provide OT faculty with a broader perspective of student issues and needs.

Faculty with Relevant Expertise

College campuses are replete with *faculty with relevant expertise*. Faculty in the areas of special education, rehabilitation, counseling, and so forth may be able to provide OT faculty with pertinent resources including literature or local contacts in specific disability areas such as learning disabilities. These individuals may provide content area expertise, but when dealing with specific student issues OT faculty should work through institutional channels, such as the OSD, to protect student confidentiality.

Summary

In this chapter we have examined institutional structures, resources, and supports that may be of assistance to OT faculty as they scrutinize program practices with OT students with disabilities. We recommended that OT faculty investigate specific campus structures and make efforts to communicate and align with other campus access initiatives and activities to promote the successful development, implementation, and ongoing review of OT policies pertaining to students with disabilities. We will now turn our attention to specific activities within the OT program including defining essential OT requirements (chapter 3) and determining reasonable accommodations (chapter 4).

• • •

References

Brown v. Washington University, CA No. 88-1907-C-5 (Settled) 1990.

Heyward, S., Lawton, & Associates. (Eds.). (1995a). Faculty members and service providers: The unhappy alliance. *Disability Accommodation Digest, 4* (3,4), 3.

Melaville, A., Blank, M., & Aseyesh, C. (1993). *Together we can.* Washington, DC: U.S. Department of Education.

Scott, S. (1996). Understanding colleges: An overview of college support services and programs available to clients from transition planning through graduation. *Journal of Vocational Rehabilitation, 6,* 217–230.

Recommended Readings

Brinckerhoff, L., Shaw, S., & McGuire, J. (1993). *Promoting access to postsecondary education for students with learning disabilities.* Austin, TX: PRO-ED.

Kroeger, S., & Schuck, J. (1995). *Responding to disability issues in student affairs.* San Francisco, CA: Jossey-Bass.

Mangrum, C., & Strichart, S. (1988). *College and the learning disabled student.* Orlando, FL: Grune & Stratton.

Ryan, D., & McCarthy, M. (1994). *A student affairs guide to the ADA and disability issues.* Washington, DC: NASPA.

CHAPTER 3

When essential components are clearly and objectively delineated, a nondiscriminatory standard is established for all students.

— S. Scott, 1990

Technical Standards and Essential Requirements

Shirley Wells and Sandy Hanebrink
with contributions from
Kimberly Hartmann

A common belief is that there is a constitutional right to public education in the United States. While there is no express right to public education in the federal Constitution, the right to education is grounded in both federal and state laws, statutes, case laws, and administrative rules and regulations. Technical standards and essential requirements are among those laws that assist state and local government educational agencies and institutions to meet not only the needs of students, but also society, at all levels in the educational process—preschool, elementary, secondary, collegiate, graduate, and professional.

With the ADA and Section 504 of the Rehabilitation Act of 1973 mandating equal opportunity for individuals with disabilities in education, the need for technical standards and essential program requirements has increased. Titles II and III of the ADA specifically address admission standards, integration of the student into settings and programs, and architectural barriers. These titles have given technical standards and essential program requirements the primary function of ensuring educational access to all students. They also give "qualified" students and applicants with disabilities equal opportunities in admission, education, and services. Technical and essential requirements allow students to assess clearly their potential to complete an educational program, activity, or both.

Curriculum requirements, related licensing requirements, components of a course, and the extent to which modifications are appropriate help determine technical standards and essential program requirements. Based upon the diversity of the program, each institution must develop its own technical standards and requirements. This chapter focuses on the process of developing and writing inclusive technical standards and essential requirements that ensure full educational accessibility to all students.

Qualified Students

As the number of students and applicants seeking to attend institutions of higher education increases, colleges and universities can expect to see even more individuals with disabilities applying for admission. It is important for postsecondary institutions, as well as individual programs, to define what a "qualified student" is (or is not) (see Figure 3.1). This definition should be based on the requirements and functions of a student by an institution and its programs.

Title II of the ADA prohibits discrimination against any "qualified individual with a disability" by postsecondary institutions. It defines a qualified person as:

An individual with a disability who with or without reasonable modifications to rules, policies, or practices, the removal of architectural, communication, or transportation barriers, or the provision of auxiliary aids and services, meets the essential eligibility requirements for the receipts of services or the participation in programs or activities provided by a public entity. (28 CFR 35.104 [Title II of ADA])

Careful analysis is needed to determine whether an individual by definition is an "individual with a disability" and/or is "qualified." Those individuals who meet these definitions are protected by Title II of the ADA.

People commonly refer to disabilities or disabling conditions in a broad sense. For example, poverty or lack of education may impose real limitations on an individual's opportunities. Likewise, being only 5 feet in height may prove to be an insurmountable barrier to an individual whose ambition is to play professional basketball. Although one might loosely characterize these conditions as "disabilities" in relation to the aspirations of the particular individual, the disabilities reached by Title II are limited to those that meet the ADA's legal definition — those that place substantial limitations on an individual's major activities (ADA Title II Technical Manual).

Title II protects three categories of individuals with disabilities:

1. Individuals who have a physical or mental impairment that substantially limits one or more major life activities.

2. Individuals who have a record of a physical or mental impairment that substantially limits one or more of the individual's major life activities.

3. Individuals with or who are regarded as having such an impairment, whether they have the impairment or not. Physical impairments include physiological disorders or conditions, cosmetic disfigurement, and anatomical loss. Specific examples of physical impairments include orthopedic, visual, speech, and hearing impairments; cerebral palsy; epilepsy; muscular dystrophy; multiple sclerosis; cancer; heart disease; diabetes; HIV disease; tuberculosis; drug addiction; and alcoholism. Mental impairments include mental or psychological disorders such as mental retardation, organic brain syndrome, or emotional or

mental illness, and specific learning disabilities (ADA Title II Technical Manual).

The ADA specifically excludes from the definition of disability: transvestism, transsexualism, pedophilia, exhibitionism, voyeurism, gender identity disorders not resulting from physical impairments, other sexual behavior disorders, compulsive gambling, kleptomania, pyromania, and psychoactive substance use disorders resulting from current illegal use of drugs (28 CFR 35.104).

In a *senior staff memorandum* (1992), the U.S. Department of Education Office for Civil Rights (OCR) clarified the distinctions among "having a disability," having a "record of a disability" and being "regarded as having a disability." OCR states:

… in order to be entitled to academic adjustments and auxiliary aids, the student must currently have a disability that substantially limits a major life activity. The other two categories merely protect the student from being discriminated against for this reason.

An institution of higher education generally cannot make inquiries about the existence of a student's disability prior to admission (ADA, 34 CFR, 104.42[b][4]); *Albany Medical College*, 1993; *University of Medicine & Dentistry of New Jersey*, 1993; *West Georgia College*, 1995).

A student with a disability may not be refused admission if he or she meets the requisite technical and academic standards for admission or participation in the university's program or activity (Section 504.34, CFR 104.3.[k][3]). Some individuals with disabilities contend that postsecondary institutions discriminate against applicants with disabilities because their GPA and/or SAT scores or similar standardized entrance examination scores reflect their disabilities and not their skills and knowledge. However, the OCR has consistently upheld the rights of institutions to set admission standards (*Halasz v. University of New England*, 1993; *The Medical College of Pennsylvania*, 1994).

In *Southeastern Community College v. Davis* (1979), a U.S. Supreme Court decision held that the college did not discriminate against a student with a serious hearing impairment when it denied her admission to its nursing program. The court concluded that the student was not "otherwise qualified" because she could not effectively participate in clinical courses without individualized supervision by an instructor. Such supervision and/or lowering of program requirements to allow access goes beyond the "reasonable accommodation" requirements of Section 504. OCR has affirmed that institutions are under no obligation to alter their standards in order to accommodate students with disabilities (Kincaid, 1995).

Technical Standards

Technical standards are defined as "all nonacademic criteria that are essential to participate in the program in question" (34 CFR Part 104 Appendix A, paragraph [5]). These are admission requirements other than SAT and/or GPAs that must be met by all students admitted to the program. These qualification standards may include personal and professional attributes, skills, experiences, education, physical, medical, safety, and other requirements that an individual must meet in order to be eligible for admission to the institution and program as well as the desired professional field of practice. Section 504 states:

*academic requirements that the recipient can demonstrate are essential to the program of instruction being pursued by such student or to any directly related licensing requirement will not be regarded as discriminatory (*Section 504, 104.44).

Essential eligibility requirements for participation and/or admission may be minimal or stringent. Criteria for admission can be objective or subjective in nature. Yet they must be nondiscriminatory and related to the essential nature of the program. Admission criteria such as volunteer and/or paid work experiences with people with disabilities, essays, interviews, letters of recommendations, or cardiopulmonary resuscitation (CPR) certification should not only be related to the essential nature of the program, but also be defendable by the institution and program as essential requirements. In *Mills College* (1991), OCR determined that the college's admission criteria included objective and subjective items that were nondiscriminatory

when an applicant alleged that she was denied admission based on a "perceived disability" of mental illness:

The Admission Committee considered 12 factors in addition to SAT *scores and* GPA. *Factors such as her withdrawal from four of six classes, five of which were nonacademic, and weak reference letters were decisive.*

Yet, an institution may not impose standards or selection criteria for participation in its programs, services, or activities that either screen out or tend to screen out persons with disabilities, unless it can show that such requirements are necessary for the provision of the service, program, or activity (28 CFR 35.130 [Title II], 29 CFR 1630.4 [Title I]). In the case of *Pennsylvania State University* (1991), OCR found the university as having violated Section 504's regulations by:

(a)   The use of preadmission inquiries.

(b)   The use of a test or criterion for admission that has a disproportionately adverse effect on persons with disabilities.

(c)   The use of a medical examination to determine the presence of a disability upon receipt of an application or inquiry from anyone who had been previously incarcerated or had a history of emotional or behavioral problems.

Any inquiries regarding the presence of a physical or mental condition that could interfere with the applicant's ability to graduate from the school or prevent the applicant from being employed after graduation violate Section 504 and the ADA. Any eligibility standard that has an adverse impact on individuals with disabilities must be "necessary or essential" to the program.

Overall technical standards must:

- Be nonacademic eligibility requirements

- Be requisite for admission

- Evolve from the essential function of the program

- Apply to all students

- Not be established to discriminate for or against a person with a disability, and

- Ensure that a student can benefit from the program and/or its activities.

Determining Technical Standards

Although there are not set procedures for determining and developing "eligibility" standards, a starting place may include, but is not limited to, a review of the (a) institution's admission requirements and standards, (b) professional documents and requirements such as *The Essentials of an Accredited Occupational Therapy Program* (AOTA, 1991) (professional and technical levels) and *Uniform Terminology* (AOTA, 1996), and (c) licensure requirements. For professional programs, it is important to investigate whether there are mandated physical and/or cognitive requirements for that profession. This can be done through the professional organization and/or licensing (state or national) bodies. A variety of resources and input from the faculty, 504 coordinator/OSD, legal personnel, and other students should be used throughout the process.

It does not violate the law to require individuals with disabilities to meet legitimate standards and criteria. However, legitimate safety requirements/criteria can be imposed only if they are based on real risks, not on speculation, stereotypes, or generalizations about individuals with disabilities. OCR upheld the right of the *University of North Carolina at Greensboro* (1995) to reject the application of a student with a criminal history who failed to provide current psychological and clinical evaluation results to respond to questions concerning whether he posed a direct threat to the safety of the campus. The applicant acknowledged in his application that he had committed a crime, but contended that it was related to his disability, schizophrenia. The purpose of this provision is to ensure that individuals with disabilities are not excluded from opportunities unless they are actually unable to participate and benefit from the program.

Technical standards should be related to the essential function of the program. They are not to be used to exclude an individual with a disability if that individual can satisfy the criteria with the provision of a reasonable accommodation. Professional terminology and/or jargons should not be used in the standards. Each criterion must be clearly written. A technical standard for all students might say:

The student, with or without reasonable accommodation, must be able to demonstrate academic readiness at the postsecondary level by:

- Meeting the minimum GPA and prerequisite coursework applicable at the time of application.

- Documenting volunteer and/or paid work experience with people with disabilities.

- Submitting all required letters of recommendation within the required time frame.

- Having the ability to participate in the admission process involving one day on campus activities, including an interview, group task, and reading and writing tests.

- Having a working and/or basic knowledge of the philosophy and functions of an occupational therapy practitioner.

- Having the ability to communicate effectively both orally and in writing, using appropriate grammar, vocabulary, and word usage, and

- Knowing the difference between the profession of occupational therapy and other allied health professions (physical, recreation, and speech therapies, etc.).

Title II of the ADA provides protection against discrimination in the administration of tests (28 CFR 35.140). Any tests and/or activities used during the selection process should be reviewed to ensure that they measure the applicant's skills and/or aptitude or whatever they purport to measure, rather than the applicant's visual, speaking, or manual skills (unless the test is designed to measure hearing, visual, speaking or manual skills).

Once the technical standards and criteria are written, it should be ascertained as to whether they are "necessary or essential." According to Heyward (1995), several pertinent questions should be asked about each admission or eligibility standard:

- Is it necessary with respect to proper identification of program participants?

- Is it necessary with respect to maintaining the essential nature of the program?

- Does the program design or implementation clearly reflect the essential nature of the criterion/standard?

- Is there a "logical correlation between program goals and purposes and the restrictions or conditions imposed?"

"Necessary or essential" eligibility standards should not be waived. If they can be waived then they are not essential to the program. Even if the standards are "necessary or essential," reasonable accommodations that permit individuals to satisfy the requirements of the standards must be provided.

When the standards are completed, a review process by a variety of agencies, organizations, and individuals should be initiated. Groups to include in this process may be the institution's advisory board, administrators for academic and student affairs, 504 coordinator, and faculty. Representatives of fieldwork personnel and students as well as community individuals also may be included. Some possible questions to ask during this review process are:

- Are the standards directly linked to the essential requirements of the program?

- Can the essential nature of the standards be defended, if necessary?

- Do the standards screen out or exclude a disproportionate number of individuals with disabilities or persons from a particular race, gender, or national origin?

- Can the standards be met with or without reasonable accommodation?

- If the standards cannot be met with reasonable accommodation or exclude a class of people, can they be defended?

A periodic review of the technical standards should be a part of the program's ongoing self-evaluation and analysis. The following section provides examples of technical standards.

Samples of Technical Standards and Essential Program Requirements

Program Minimum Skills for Eligibility to Participate in Educational Programs and Activities

The following skills are needed by applicants to this program. Applicants and students should possess these abilities, or with the help of compensatory techniques and/or assistive devices, be able to demonstrate the ability to become proficient.

1. Standard cognitive ability.

2. Ability to use therapeutic communication
   - attending
   - clarifying
   - coaching
   - facilitating
   - touching.

3. Physical strength necessary to:
   - position another person
   - assist in a transfer
   - perform range of motion exercises

- perform CPR

(or cognitive ability to instruct an assistant to perform these activities).

4. Ability to measure
   - another person's body (range, strength, cardiopulmonary status, reflexes, developmental level, etc.)
   - another person's psychological, cognitive, and perceptual status
   - using a variety of treatment modalities

(or cognitive ability to instruct an assistant to perform these activities).

5. Manual dexterity to
   - grasp
   - push
   - pull
   - hold
   - cut

(or cognitive ability to instruct an assistant to perform these activities).

6. Ability to function (consult, negotiate, share) as part of a team.

7. Ability to operate and maintain equipment (e.g., orthotic, assistive technology, modality equipment) or cognitive ability to instruct an assistant to perform these activities.

Note. This document is pending legal approval. Reprinted with permission.

University of Minnesota Programs in Occupational and Physical Therapy: Clinical/Fieldwork Environment Checklist

Center Name:
Clinical Area (OT or PT, and Phys Dis, Psych, School, etc): Completed by:

Check those factors which may indicate problem areas for a student with a disability.

I. Continuing Ed Location
( ) Indoor
( ) Outdoor
( ) Both I/O
( ) Floor Level
( ) Other

II. Mobility
( ) Steps
( ) Narrow Aisles
( ) Slick Floors
( ) Carpeted Floors
( ) Steep Grades
( ) Protrusions
( ) Narrow Doorways (less than 32 in.)
( ) Elevator Accessibility
( ) Ground Level Entrance
( ) Parking
( ) Curb Ramps & Walks
( ) Ramps
( ) Handrails for Ramps
( ) Handrails for Stairways
( ) Other

III. Restroom Facilities
( ) Toilet Rooms Accessible
( ) Toilet Stalls Accessible
( ) Grab Bars Provided
( ) Dispensers Accessible
( ) Toilet Stool for Handicapped
( ) Sink Height
( ) Faucet Handles
( ) Lockers
( ) Other

IV. Physical Design
( ) Room Dimensions
( ) Furniture Placement
( ) Equipment/Materials Placement
( ) Table Heights
( ) Equipment Tools
( ) Power Switch Locations
( ) Floor Covering
( ) Pathways
( ) Proximity of Others
( ) Windows
( ) Obstacles

( ) Counter Heights
( ) Door Handles
( ) Seating
( ) Sinks/Soap Dispensers
( ) Other

V. Hazards
( ) Safety–General
( ) Electrical
( ) Mechanical
( ) Height
( ) Radiant Energy
( ) Explosives
( ) Toxic or Caustic Chemical
( ) Noise/Vibration
( ) Other

VI. Atmospheric Conditions
( ) Temperature Extremes
( ) Wet/Humid
( ) Drafts
( ) Fumes
( ) Odors
( ) Dust
( ) Poor Ventilation
( ) Gases
( ) Allergy Inducing
( ) Other

VII. General
( ) Accessible Water Fountain
( ) Signage Indicating Accessible Facilities
( ) Elevator Equipped with Audio or Tactile Controls
( ) Public Telephone Accessible
( ) Warning Signal
( ) Fire Escape
( ) Lighting
( ) Cafeteria Accessible
( ) Other

Note. From the National Rehabilitation Hospital, Washington, D.C. Adapted with permission.

University of Minnesota Occupational Therapy Student Performance Essentials and Critical Demands (4/15/93)

Didactic Preparation

Following completion of the didactic and clinical fieldwork experience the student will perform at the competency of an entry-level occupational therapist (see AOTA document), with or without accommodations.

- Attends class approximately 35+ hours per week which included the following:

  - lectures
  - laboratory
  - task group meetings
  - integrated clinical experience

- Meets class standards for course completion

- Participates in classroom discussions

- Performs* or instructs** others in a timely manner in the following:

  - transfers—performs or instructs
  - activities of daily living (dependent through independent status) performs and instructs
  - splinting–performs
  - therapeutic activities/procedures–performs
  - task and verbal group activities–performs
  - assessment procedures–performs

- Uses sound judgment and safety precautions.

- Applies critical thinking process to require ments of the academic learning experience:

  - lecture
  - laboratory
  - integrated clinical experience

- Follows standard stated in student progress handbook

- Addresses problems or questions to the appropriate person at the appropriate time

- Maintains classroom work area, equipment, and supplies

- Maintains personal appearance and hygiene conducive to professional student setting

- Moves to various locations required for classes

Direct performance of activity/procedure by student or student teaching patient/client how to perform activity/procedure.

**Student instructs someone other than patient/client (caregiver or another team member).*

In an average academic day a student must:

Sit	2-6 hours
Walk/Travel	2 hours

The following requirements are included in classroom activities:

- *50 pounds* is the heaviest weight *lifted* while sitting or standing in one place

- *25 pounds* is the heaviest weight *carried* while moving/traveling up to 50 feet

- *25 pounds* is the heaviest force *exerted* to push/pull objects up to 50 feet

Clinical Fieldwork Experience

- Physical activity is center dependent (refer to each center's file)

- Travels to clinical fieldwork site

- Moves within clinic/community setting

- Follows appropriate chain of command

- Follows all policies and procedures required by setting

- Completes all assignments

Key:	
Rarely = 1–10%	
Occasionally = 11– 33%	
Frequently = 34– 66%	
Continuously = 67–100%	

The student is required throughout the 5-quarter academic program to:

Lift less than 10 pounds	F
Lift 10–25 pounds	O
Lift 25–50 pounds	R
Twist	F
Bend/Stoop	O
Squat	O
Climb stools	R
Reach above shoulder level	O
Kneel	R
Push/Pull	O
Use hand repetitively	C
Simple grasping	C
Firm grasp	O
Manual dexterity	F
Finger dexterity (manipulation of objects less than 1 in.)	F
Coordinate verbal/manual instruction	F
Use auditory/tactile/visual senses to evaluate status of an individual	F

- Maintains patient/client confidentiality

- Complies with dress code

- Meets attendance requirements

- Demonstrates professional standards of practice and adheres to code of ethics

- Maintains work area, equipment, and supplies in a manner conducive to efficiency and safety

- Models socially appropriate behaviors

- Manages time effectively

- Creates an environment which maximizes patient's/client's responses

- Documents all required information

- Effectively adjusts communication for intended audience

- Communicates with patients, families, staff, coworkers, and other health professionals effectively and professionally

- Demonstrates problem-solving skills in patient care

- Gathers information needed prior to assessment

- Selects relevant areas to assess

- Selects the correct methods for assessment

- Administers assessment procedures accurately

- Adapts assessment method as needed

- Interprets assessment data accurately

- Interprets assessment/reassessment results accurately and completely

- Establishes relevant goals/outcomes and treatment plan with patient/client

Note. From the University of Minnesota. Reprinted with permission.

Lourdes College OTA Program

Lourdes College is a Catholic liberal arts institution of higher education in the Franciscan tradition. It seeks to serve men and women in an atmosphere of respect for the individual and care for the whole person. It commits itself to provide that environment for all students who enroll there. The ADA bans discrimination against persons with disabilities. In keeping with this law, Lourdes College makes every effort to ensure quality education for all of its students. The following document fulfills the obligation of the oc-cupational therapy assistant OTA program to inform students of the essential functions demanded by the job of a certified occupational therapy assistant (COTA) with or without accommodations.

Essential Functions of a COTA and Candidate/Student for the Lourdes College OTA Program

1. The decision to work in a health care profession should be based on an understanding of various health care professions. Some health professions require working in intense situations with very ill or severely injured people. Some require working with the mentally ill. OT practitioners work with all types of clients, therefore:

It is an essential that a candidate who wants to practice OT to have had experience working with someone with a disability and have a desire to help alleviate disability.

It is an essential of a student in the OTA program to be able to render assistance to individuals of all cultures, across the lifespan, without prejudice or repulsion.

It is an essential that a student and practitioner be able to establish therapeutic interpersonal relationships centered on the needs of the client and cooperative interpersonal relationships with colleagues centered on issues and/or tasks.

2. Critical to the selection of a profession is the understanding of what the profession is, and what the professional does. Not everyone is suited to a certain profession, therefore:

An essential of a candidate for the OTA program is knowing the difference between the profession of OT and other allied health professions (PT, recreation, social work, speech, etc.).

An essential of a student in the OTA program is knowing the basic functions of the profession and agreeing with the basic philosophy and practice of occupational therapy.

3. OT is a communication profession. Practitioners are required to communicate and build relationships with individuals of all ages, races, sexes, and cultural differences. They are also required to communicate in groups. They should have an interest in several subjects in order to converse on a casual and therapeutic basis regarding a client's personal values, interests, environmental challenges, lifestyle preferences, and perceptions of a performance therefore:

> An essential of a candidate for the OTA program is the ability to communicate effectively both orally and in writing, using appropriate grammar, vocabulary, and word usage.

> An essential of a student in the OTA program is prior experience working with groups or clubs and the willingness to deal with even the most difficult people to get the job done.

> An essential of a student in the OTA program is the ability to consult with others as necessary, report findings to appropriate persons, foster col legial relationships, and instruct others.

4. OT is a medically related profession. Consistent performance of duties is of major concern. Personal problems, health problems, and other employment, regardless of the nature, cannot interfere with the performance of assignments and class/clinic attendance. Students are responsible for their own transportation to and from fieldwork modules in each course and Level II assignments, therefore:

> An essential of a candidate for OT is being a re sponsible individual. He/she must meet all re quirements set forth in the OTA program and all fieldwork facilities.

> An essential of a student in the OTA program is independent mobility and the ability to secure transportation to and from all college classes and fieldwork.

5. The OTA students are responsible for adhering to the policies and procedures of the college and all facilities they attend for their fieldwork assignments, therefore:

> An essential of a student in the OTA program is seeking knowledge of and abiding by all policies and procedures of the college and fieldwork sites.

6. OT departments are often located in medically related facilities which are critical of certain attire for safety and patient-care reasons, i.e., large and wild jewelry is a hazard around machinery and patients; heavy perfumes are obnoxious to clients who are ill; long hair, unprotected, is a machinery hazard. Clothing must be presentable and clean in accordance with hospital regulations, therefore:

> An essential of a student in the OTA program is dressing in accordance with recommended college policy and the policies of clinical fieldwork sites. A conservative approach to dress is recommended.

7. Health care professionals frequently engage in emergency situations. CPR and other emergency training is required of practitioners of occupational therapy, therefore:

> An essential of a candidate for the OTA and the COTA is the ability to respond appropriately in emergency situations, to make quick decisions under sometimes stressful situations.

> An essential of a student in the OTA program is the completion of a course in **CPR** (must have proof of this prior to the second year of OTA coursework).

8. Professional ethics is the rightness and wrongness in relation to performing duties and responsibilities of a profession. Ethical behavior is influenced by the attitudes and values an individual has in relationship to carrying out their duties and responsibilities, therefore:

An essential of a candidate for the OTA program and the practicing COTA is a set of ethical behaviors that will allow them to be receptive to professional ethics teaching in order to practice in a health care setting.

An essential of a candidate for the program is a sense of rightness and wrongness in a health care setting.

An essential of a student in the OTA program is behavior that demonstrates honesty and integrity—plagiarized work will be dealt with by immediate dismissal from the program.

9. OT practitioners must be certified by the American Occupational Therapy Certification Board and licensed to practice in the state of Ohio. Several other states also require a license. The Licensure Boards certify professional competence and moral character required to provide medically related treatment to the consumer. A person convicted of a felony may be denied a seat for the certification or licensure in Ohio or other states, therefore:

An essential of a candidate for the OTA program is that the person should not have a conviction of a felonious nature that will make them ineligible to sit for the national certification examination for OTAs or to attain state licensure.

It is essential for a student in the OTA program to disclose felony convictions to the program director.

10. OT practitioners must be physically coordinated and able to handle moving clients or direct same in many practice settings. Visual observation equity is also necessary to observe client nonverbal behavior to ensure safety in the clinic, therefore:

An essential of a candidate is adequate physical strength to perform lifting and patient transfers.

It is essential for a student in the program to have functional coordination and vision and be independent in mobility.

Other physical performance standards and job essentials required of OTA students and practicing COTAs with or without reasonable accommodations are outlined in the attached grid.

Lourdes College
Occupational Therapy Assistance Program

I have read and understand the Essential Functions document for being a student in the OTA program and practitioner in the profession of OT.

Signed   Date

Please return this page with your application to the OTA program.

Note. From Lourdes College. Reprinted with permission.

Essential Program Requirements

Allied health programs must review their admission criteria and standards and document the essential functions that they expect of each student. The term *essential function* is a key concept referred to in Title I of the ADA. Essential functions are those considered to be necessary or fundamental to performance of a job. In postsecondary education, the student's job is to learn and participate in an academic environment and the clinical/fieldwork environment as well. If a student cannot meet the designated essential functions with reasonable accommodations, the institution or program is under no obligation to enroll that student (Meyers & Ellingham, 1994) (see Table 3.1).

The critical question in providing reasonable accommodation is to determine the essential curriculum requirements, the methods components of a course, and the extent to which modifications are appropriate for a student with a disability. In health care programs, essential requirements are those requisites that the institution and program, licensure and certification boards, and the profession respectively have determined to be critical in (a) meeting the competencies, goals, and purpose of the program, and (b) maintaining the safety of the people served in the educational process and eventually in the therapeutic arena. The term *essential requirements* in health care professional programs means not only the fundamental responsibilities and functions of all students in the postsecondary institution but also the essential functions of individuals within the profession. Both of these areas must be taken into account by professional programs such as occupational therapy education programs when establishing essential program requirements.

The goal of essential program requirements is to clearly state the aspects and requirements of the academic coursework, laboratory activities, and fieldwork placement. These essential program requirements are fundamental to obtaining the competencies necessary for a practitioner. They aid all students to explicitly understand what is expected throughout the program. Clarity and conciseness are critical for faculty, fieldwork personnel, potential students, as well as current students, to understand the expectations of students admitted and enrolled in the program.

Establishing Essential Program Requirements

While it is the right of institutions to establish the essential components of their own individual programs, it is also each institution's responsibility to defend the components as actually being essential. Therefore, establishing essential program requirements is very important to the institution, program, and students. *It is something that should not be taken lightly.* It is a process that takes time, analysis, and discussion. There are certain points that should be kept in mind throughout the process:

- This process will take time, analysis, and discussion, and possibly compromise.

- As the program, curriculum, objectives, or the institution itself changes, so may the essential requirements.

- The process will require a collaborative effort by the department and institution.

- Embedded within the process are matters related to the college or institution's administration, disabled student services office, and legal counsel.

- The goal of the process should be reviewed frequently to provide guidance on ensuring equal opportunity for all qualified students.

Identifying the Essential Functions of the Program

In order to establish essential program requirements, one should first identify the essential functions of the individual program. The essential program requirements of an individual program should represent an integration of the institution's philosophy, the profession's essentials of an accredited educational program, and the program's philosophy and curriculum design. The mission and philosophy of the institution and program provide the answer as to why the particular program exists. Accreditation essentials generally provide the foundation for all aspects of the educational program including administration, resources, personnel, facility space, and curriculum to ensure that the program is capable of guiding graduates toward professional competencies. And the curriculum design gives the description and evidence of certain essential skills.

Determining Essential Components

The purpose of the program, institution, or profession and the outcome variables that are absolutely required of all students should initially direct the focus of the essentials (see Table 3.1). Whether the program exists for a specific purpose should be addressed (e.g., OT educational programs exist to prepare individuals to function as occupational therapy practitioners). The degree of expertise or skill required to perform the component is another factor to explore. The

Table 3.1
Guidelines for Determining Essential Components of a Course or Program

I.   What is the purpose of the program?

II. What outcome variables are absolutely required of all participants?

    A. Program
       1. What are the skills or competencies required in the field after graduation?
       2. What are the requirements for licensing or professional accreditation?

    B. Course
       1. What academic skills must be demonstrated?
       2. What percentage of subject area knowledge must be mastered?
       3. What specific knowledge, principles, or concepts must be mastered?

III. What methods of instruction are nonnegotiable? Why?
    (For example, auditory presentation of musical compositions may be deemed
    absolutely necessary in a music appreciation class because of the designated nature
    and purpose of the course.)

IV. What methods of assessing outcome variables are absolutely necessary? Why?
    (For example, a nursing student's proficiency in starting an IV must be assessed by
    physical performance because of skill development required by the major and/or
    licensing requirements.)

V.   What are acceptable levels of performance on these measures?
    (For example, 100% of program competencies must be demonstrated; 85% of exam
    questions must be answered or performed correctly.)

Note. From "Coming to terms with the otherwise qualified student with a learning disability," by S.S. Scott, 1990. *Journal of Learning Disabilities, 23,* 398-405. Reprinted with permission.

consequences of not having a component may be another indicator of whether a particular component is essential. In a professional educational program, the actual work experiences of people who have performed or are currently performing as practitioners provide pragmatic evidence of the duties and components that are essential. Whether a particular function is essential is a factual determination that must be made by each individual program and/or institution. All relevant information should be considered—mission of the institution, accreditation requirements, licensure requirements, and current practice requirements.

Writing Essential Program Requirements

The delineation of the essentials of a program need not involve creating entirely new requirements. Existing documents such as course syllabi, laboratory learning objectives, and fieldwork objectives can provide a strong foundation upon which to build. The expected or desired outcomes of the program from all educational domains including knowledge, skills, judgments, and attitude should be explored and discussed.

Not all outcomes are essential to the program (Table 3.2). Some may be mandated by the postsecondary institution, some may be ideal outcomes that would maximize the learning potential of students or enhance the quality of the education, and some may be mandated by the accreditation and credentialing agencies as well as licensing bodies.

Table 3.2
Examples of Outcomes Criteria

- Outcomes that meet the documents of the profession
- Outcomes that reflect the individual nature of the program
- Outcomes that are expected at entry level
- Outcomes of the program
- Outcomes for the major activities of the program such as courses, labs, or fieldwork experiences

---

The methods of instruction and assessment to be used in the program also must be analyzed. Several fundamental questions should be asked during this process:

- Are the methods of instruction negotiable?
- Can an alternative method of instruction be considered for assessing essential outcomes?
- How will alternative measures be evaluated?
- What are acceptable levels of mastery in each course, lab, or field placement?
- What are acceptable levels of performance on an alternative measure?

Faculty members should analyze their methods of instruction and assessment for acceptable alternatives to be accomplished with or without reasonable accommodation. They also need to decide whether the methods are absolutely critical or essential to the course and program.

It is important to note that the inquiry into essential functions, requirements, and components is not intended to lower standards. It is used to show that programs and institutions impose such requirements on all students, disabled and nondisabled. This is applicable to all types of criteria including safety, vision, hearing, walking, lifting, and testing requirements.

An example of determining a essential requirement may be:

A program has determined that an essential function of an occupational therapy student is to move a client from a sitting position in a chair to a sitting position on a mat. This task has a physical requirement of the ability to lift and move a 70- to 200-pound weight. This standard is profession related. However, it would be a reasonable accommodation to eliminate this standard for an otherwise qualified student who could not move a client because of a disability, if other people are available to help.

The essential program requirement may be:

The student must have the ability to move, or instruct someone how to move, a client ... or the student, with or without reasonable accommodation, must be able to move a client ...

Determining Clinical and Fieldwork Requirements

When determining clinical and fieldwork essential requirements, issues such as safety, therapeutic interactions, and documentation should be considered (*Blackhawk Technical College*, 1995, *Bucks County Area Vocational-Technical School*, 1995; *California State University*, 1993; *Mary Baldwin College*, 1994). Academic and clinical educators must be involved in the determination of clinical and fieldwork essential requirements. They, too, should result in an outcome that provides information to potential and current students and serves as a guide for faculty, staff, and clinical educators (see Tables 3.2 and 3.3).

Reviewing and documenting the accessibility and conditions of the clinical site, in additional to defining essential functions, provide students with information about the environmental conditions at the site (University of Minnesota, Programs in Occupational and Physical Therapy, Clinical/Fieldwork Environment Checklist). If students provide input to their choice of fieldwork sites, current environmental information would assist students in determining their need for reasonable accommodation. This information can be maintained in central files along with other information about the site that is accessible to all students. (See chapter 4 for further information on accommodations in field placement.)

Samples of Essential Program Requirements

Texas Woman's University
Denton/Dallas/Houston, Texas

School of Occupational Therapy
P. O. Box 425648
Denton, TX 76204-5648
Phone: 817-898-2802
Fax: 817-898-2486

General Outline for Essential Elements for Occupational Therapy

I. Academic Readiness — The student, with or without reasonable accommodation, must be able to:

A. Demonstrate eligibility for scholarship at the postsecondary level by:

1. Satisfying general admission requirements of the Texas Woman's University.

2. Satisfying specific admission require ments unique to the School of Occupational Therapy, including:

a.* GPA/GRE (if required): the minimum GPA/GRE applicable at the time of application;

b.* observation or volunteer work in occupational therapy; and

c.* participation in the admission process involving one day on campus.

3.* Having the ability to be independently mobile within classroom buildings and to various field sites.

B.* Demonstrate the ability to profit from advanced scholarship by:

1.* Maintaining outgoing communication with assigned academic advisor and other faculty as appropriate.

2. Planning an academic schedule appropriate to the content area selected as a major.

C.* Demonstrate eligibility to practice as a clinical occupational therapy student through adaptive attitudes and personal skills including:

1.* Computer literacy at a level sufficient for word processing and institutional documentation.

2.* Manual dexterity sufficient to manipulate evaluation and treatment equipment, after proper instruction, including but not limited to: hand tools for working in wood, leather, ceramics, fibers and plastics; computer disks and various operating switches; and standardized testing equipment and materials as appropriate to activities including self-care, work, and leisure.

3.* Hearing and visual acuity sufficient to respond independently to an emergency situation signaled by a change in a individual's appearance, pulse, blood pressure, and/or by an individual's verbal or physical communication of distress.

4.* Ability to lift 15 lbs. independently and to place objects of this weight at various levels including floor level and overhead.

5.* Ability to perform 50% of a physical transfer of a patient up to 200 lbs. with assistance or with assistive devices, i.e., from a wheelchair to toilet or tub while maintaining good body mechanics.

6.* Ability to work within clinical environments which involve exposure to persons with physical and mental disabilities; and to pain, grief, death, stress, communicable diseases, blood and body fluids, and toxic substances.

7.* Ability to work with a diverse patient population including persons of various ages, ethnic, racial, religious, and socioeconomic backgrounds.

II. Academic Progress — The student, with or without reasonable accommodation, must be able to:

A. Profit from learning experiences relevant to the occupational therapy curriculum including such means as:

1.* Attending scheduled class lectures, laboratory sessions, testing situations, and fieldwork.

2.* Communicating in person to exchange accurate information on a one-to-one basis, in a small group, large classroom setting, or large group.

3.* Communicating by completing written assignments in standard and organized English such that 60 words can be produced in 15 minutes.

4. Satisfying specific course and program objectives as specified in the syllabi.

5. Maintaining a satisfactory GPA during progression of the program as specified in the catalog.

B. Demonstrate critical thinking skills deemed appropriate for the academic level and discipline content, including such means as:

1. Successfully completing the core curriculum if applicable.

2. Comprehending appropriate professional literature as evidenced by analysis and syn-thesis of professional literature in written assignments and classroom presentations.

3. Articulating information specific to the academic major.

4. Modifying behavior/performance in the classroom or the clinic after feedback from the instructor or clinical supervisor.

5.* Problem solving ability sufficient to organize and complete multiple tasks such as various homework assignment accurately and within assigned time frames.

C. Demonstrate eligibility to assume a professional role at program completion, including such means as:

1. Meeting all matriculation requirements specific to the academic program.

2.* Completing the following with documentation to TWU Student Health Services prior to Level I fieldwork courses:

   a.* immunizations as required by the state of Texas,

   b.* Hepatitis B immunization or a signed waiver or a physician's statement, and

   c.* annual TB test.

3.* Purchasing group liability insurance and maintaining this throughout the program.

4. Demonstrating clinically appropriate judgment, safety precautions, and teamwork during lecture and laboratory sessions.

5. Successfully completing all Level I fieldwork.

6. Completing Level II fieldwork to American Occupational Therapy Association standards.

7. Completing professional project, if required.

8.* Accepting responsibility for completion of certification and licensure requirements.

III. Conduct Within the Academy — The student, with or without reasonable accommodation, must be able to:

A. Demonstrate behaviors appropriate to study at the postsecondary level, including such means as:

1. Abiding by the current University policies for student conduct.

2. Interacting appropriately with peers, faculty, and the professional community.

B.* Demonstrate ethical behaviors including honesty as demonstrated by completing homework independently as assigned with proper use and acknowledgment of reference or other sources, and as demonstrated by independent test-taking.

Elements specific to occupational therapy

Note. From Texas Woman's University. Reprinted with permission.

College of St. Scholastica
Duluth, Minnesota
Occupational Therapy Department
Contract of Professional Behaviors

The College of St. Scholastica Graduate Programs Policy Manual outlines the responsibilities and rights of students and professors. They are as follows:

Professor Responsibilities
and Student Rights

1. Treat students with respect, regardless of their level of performance.

2. Apprise students of any changes in the curriculum that could affect them.

3. Inform students about Graduate Studies policies and grievance procedures.

4. Provide students with honest feedback regarding their progress/level of performance.

5. Distribute graded work and performance evaluations in such a way that student's rights to privacy are maintained.

6. Provide students with information about standards and requirements for individual courses including evaluation measures.

7. Be available to help students during office hours.

8. Provide students with the opportunity to anonymously evaluate the course contents and teaching style.

9. Provide students with the opportunity to review their academic file.

10. Provide access to an advisor at least once a quarter.

Student Responsibilities With or Without Reasonable Accommodations

1. Be an active learner.

2. Enroll only in courses if the prerequisites have been met or officially waived.

3. Exhibit respect toward faculty and peer learners.

4. Adhere to standards of scholarship and ethics.

5. Meet with one's advisor each quarter and to inform the advisor of any changes in academic plans.

6. Complete course and evaluation forms when requested to do so.

7. When engaged in a practicum experience, to abide by the policies, procedures, rules, and regulations of that agency.

There are other specific issues related to professional behaviors in OT that need to be addressed. Following are specific professional behaviors expected of OT students:

1. Students are expected to attend all classes (even when an exam is scheduled for the same day in another class). If unable to attend, students will call instructor before the class. If a student misses class, it is their responsibility to obtain notes and materials and to complete any missed assignments.

2. Students are expected to be on time to class. (Walking in late is very distracting to one's peers and the instructor.)

3. Students are expected to turn in assignments on time. Failure to do so may result in an altered grade on that assignment.

4. Students will refrain from personal conversations during class time. These are very distracting to one's peers and to the instructor.

5. The profession of OT requires frequent group work and problem resolution. Therefore, in group assignments, all students should pull equal weight. If one student is not doing the work, group members are encouraged to attempt to resolve concerns prior to contacting the instructor.

6. Grammar, spelling, and typos will be considered when grading written assignments.

7. Students are encouraged to participate in class discussions.

8. Cheating and plagiarism will not be tolerated. See policy.

Note. From the College of St. Scholastica, Duluth, Minnesota. Reprinted with permission.

Essential Functions

In order to successfully complete the OTA Program at Lasell College, the student is expected to with or without reasonable accommodation:

1. Earn a minimum of a "C" grade in all OTA courses and maintain a cumulative grade point average of 2.0.

2. Handle the stresses of an intensive training program by demonstrating effective and adequate coping skills.

3. Participate fully in the academic and clinical portions of the program with reasonable accommodation, if necessary, that does not disrupt either the academic integrity of the program or the clinical authenticity of the fieldwork sites.

4. Comprehend and use the English language in an understandable manner both verbally and in writing.

5. Communicate effectively, efficiently, and appropriately with peers, faculty, supervisors, other professionals, clients, and their significant others.

6. Exhibit a spirit of cooperation and respect for peers, faculty, supervisors, other professionals, clients, and their significant others.

7. Demonstrate good observational skills and awareness of nonverbal communication.

8. Be sensitive to and understanding of client/patient needs.

9. Respect the confidentiality of client/patient information.

10. Use professional terminology correctly.

11. Demonstrate adequate documentation skills.

12. Acquire the skills to apply the principles and practices of OT.

13. Demonstrate sensorimotor skills, mobility, and general endurance necessary for the implementation of treatment techniques.

14. Apply effective teaching, dyadic, and group skills.

Note. From Lasell College. Reprinted with permission.

Documentation

Good faith efforts to comply with the intent and spirit of the law should be documented as standards and essentials are developed (see Table 3.3). Detailed written documentation must be provided to support decisions that result in students being denied access, opportunities, and benefits. The *documentation of the process* should include a listing of the persons involved, dates of meetings, and the steps taken to determine the essentials and standards. The criteria used for determining the standards and what is essential should be recorded. These may include: (a) any particular document (e.g., Essentials of an Educational Program; Uniform Terminology), (b) literature of best practices, (c) the program and institution's mission and philosophy, and (d) the licensure laws.

The *final product document* is a listing of the technical standards and essential requirements for the entire program including courses, labs, and field placement. This final document should denote (a) *when* (date) the standards and essentials were established; (b) *who* was involved in the process; (c) *what* official bodies have approved the standards and essentials; and (d) *when* the standards and essential will be reviewed. The format of the document used to inform students of the technical standards and essential program requirements may take any form — narrative, checklist, question and answer, statement of verification of ability, or a general statement informing students of the standards.

The *dissemination plan* should detail the procedures for distributing the document to the students including *when* and *how* (e.g., technical standards will be mailed with all requests for applications). It should include the location of the document (e.g., disabled student services, 504 coordinator's office, occupational therapy department, admission department, student handbook, etc.) for public access. Finally, the *review plan* should outline the procedure for any review, revision, and/or adaptation needs including time frames.

Table 3.3
Needed Documentation

- Document the process used to determine the standards and essentials (how).

- Document the criteria used for determining the standards and essentials (why).

- Document the people, institutional bodies, and/or external bodies involved in the process (who).

- Document the definitive standards and essentials program requirements (what).

- Document the review and revision process (when).

- Document the dissemination plan (where).

Dissemination

Whatever type of document is used, if it is not in the hands of the students, it is worthless. Disseminating the document is an important component of the process. Ensuring public access to the technical standards and essential program requirements is crucial. All students need to be made aware of the document and how to access it. Communicating this information to all applicants and students is imperative. Information about the rights and responsibilities under the ADA must be available to students and potential students.

Another major component of the dissemination process is ensuing the student's right to confidentiality under Section 504 and the ADA. These government mandates carry within them rules regarding the confidential treatment of disability-related information. The process of requesting reasonable accommodation within the constraints of these laws must also be communicated to all students. As with any documents used by the institution or program, they must be equally and readily accessible to all. Dissemination is key to the success of the entire process. Technical standards and essential program requirements information can be provided in course bulletins, student manuals, and orientation materials.

Summary

Educational administrators need to examine admissions procedures and requirements to determine if applicants are truly qualified to pursue specific types of studies or if some requirements are not useful for making admissions decisions. They need to look at ways to provide access to individuals with types of disabilities who may be interested in pursuing health professional studies, but who have functional limitations that may have excluded them from consideration before passage of the ADA. The excuse that a person might not be able to function in the job role is no longer acceptable if the individual is otherwise qualified to pursue the study program of interest.

Technical standards and essential requirements are to be determined individually by each institution and program. Based on the mission and philosophy of each institution and program, these standards and essentials are to be applied to all students equally, with or without reasonable accommodation. It is not only the right of each institution and program to establish standards and requirements but also their responsibility to ensure that they are inclusive and nondiscriminatory in accordance with current laws and regulations. Institutions and programs must be able to support that their technical standards and program requirements are necessary and essential. They must be inclusive and nondiscriminatory in nature. If a standard or requirement can be modified or exempted, then it is not essential. Standards and essential requirements are specific to each institution and program and, therefore, may change as the institution, program, and profession change.

Technical standards and essential program requirements must be established, written, communicated, and available to all applicants and students. Unless this information is disseminated to all applicants and students, it does not exist. The information is unknown and not recognized by legal enforcement agencies and courts of law. Technical standards and essential program requirements are the foundation of each educational program. From this base, institutions and their programs select qualified students who will be accepted, given the opportunity to be educated and directed toward professional competencies, and will benefit from the experience and participation.

Now that we have examined the process and necessity of technical standards and essential program requirements, it is important to address reasonable accommodations that ensure equal access to educational programs and activities for qualified applicants and students. Many assumptions about the capabilities of persons with different types of disabilities will be proven faulty once earnest efforts are made to accommodate people with disabilities. Like technical standards and essential requirements, reasonable accommodation is very individual and determined on a case by case basis. The next chapter will answer critical questions surrounding the provision of reasonable accommodations for those students with disabilities who meet all standards and essential requirements.

• • •

References

Albany Medical College, Complaint, No. 02-92-2005 (OCR Region II, 1993).

Americans with Disabilities Act (ADA). (1990). *Title II Technical Assistance Manual on Public Entities.* Washington, D.C: Government Printing Office.

American Occupational Therapy Association (AOTA). (1996). *Uniform terminology* (3rd ed.). Bethesda, MD: Author.

American Occupational Therapy Association (AOTA). (1991). *The essentials of an accredited occupational therapy program.* Bethesda, MD: Author.

Blackhawk Technical College (WI), Case No. 05-94-2176 (OCR Region V, 1995).

Bucks County Area Vocational-Technical School, Case No. 03-94-3007 (OCR Region III, 1995).

California State University, 4 NDLR, 359 Case No. 09-93-2037 (OCR Region IX, 1993).

Halasz v. University of New England, 821 F. Supp 40, 4 National Disability Law Report, 118 (D.M.E. 1993).

Heyward, S. (1995, Oct. 18). Support services for students with disabilities in postsecondary education settings [videoconference].

Kincaid, J.M. (1995). *Legal considerations for serving students with learning disabilities in institutions of higher education.* Center Barnstead, NH:

Mary Baldwin College (VA), Case No. 03-94-2106 (OCR Region III, 1994).

Meyers, C., & Ellingham, C. (1994). Potential patterns: The Americans with Disabilities: Allied health educators' responsibility and challenge. *Journal of Allied Health, 23*(3): 173–181.

Mills College Case No. 09-91-201 (OCR Region IX, 1991).

Office of Civil Rights. (1992).

Pennsylvania State University, Case No. 03-91-2020 (OCR Region III, 1991).

Scott, S. (1990). Coming to terms with the otherwise qualified student with a learning disability. *Journal of Learning Disabilities, 23*(7), 398–405.

Senior Staff Memorandum, 19 Individuals with Disabilities Education Law Report, 894.

Southeastern Community College v. Davis, 442, U.S. 397, 99 S.Ct. 2361 (1979).

The Medical College of Pennsylvania, Case No. 03-92-2014 (OCR Region III, 1994).

University of Medicine & Dentistry of New Jersey, No. 02-92-2006 (OCR Region II, 1993).

University of North Carolina at Greensboro, Case No. 04-94-2143 (OCR Region IV, 1995).

West Georgia College, Case No. 04-94-2192 (OCR Region IV, 1995).

CHAPTER 4

It is perhaps the understatement of the decade to say that the reasonable accommodation mandate is not an objective compliance standard that lends itself to simple straightforward analysis. In many respects, it is the legal equivalent of the Rubik's cube.

— S. Heyward, 1992

Auxiliary Aids, Academic Adjustments, and Reasonable Accommodations

Shirley Wells and Sandy Hanebrink
with contributions from
Kimberly Hartmann

Institutions that impose insurmountable physical or admissions barriers on students with disabilities or that fail to provide speedy access to equipment, services, and facilities needed by students with disabilities can cause the most damage in creating an accessible environment for all students. Academic accommodation has replaced inaccessible architecture as the chief area of concern on many campuses. In providing accommodations for students with disabilities, Section 504 of the ADA should be the guides.

Academic accommodation is a concept far broader than physical access and encompasses barriers to entry into programs, discriminatory policies and procedures in the administration of programs, and communication barriers that prevent full participation in programs or receipt of services. Although the law continues to evolve, one thing is clear: Legal challenges in the area of accommodations are frequent and colleges and universities are often found out of compliance. This chapter focuses on auxiliary aids, academic adjustments, and reasonable accommodations as well as issues related to the provision of accommodations.

Defining Reasonable Accommodation

The definition of reasonable accommodation focuses on equalization for people with disabilities in terms of education, employment, and access to public services and facilities. What is considered reasonable is determined on a case-by-case basis. While there are very few general "do's" that would hold true for all cases, it would be wise to adhere to the principle that, if a reasonable person would question the propriety of the actions, a closer look at the compliance under the Acts and the regulations should take place. If it looks like discrimination and feels like discrimination, it probably is discrimination (Heyward, 1992).

Adhering to the spirit as well as the letter of the law is not an easy task. It requires a balance between the interest of the individual with a disability to be included and the interest of the institution to protect the integrity of its programs. The compliance standards under both Section 504 Part 104.44 (d)(1) and the ADA (and their implementing regulations) *require an institution to take such steps as are necessary to ensure that an individual with a disability is not denied the opportunity to benefit from or participate in the institution's programs.* It is the responsibility of everyone — the institution, program, faculty, individual with a disability, and student body—to ensure that this balance occurs.

Reasonable accommodations in postsecondary education have become synonymous with academic adjustments, auxiliary aids and services, interpreters, and modifications. Decisions regarding a person with a disability should be based on the individual needs and abilities, and not generalizations regarding individuals with disabilities as a class. All legitimate alternatives should be considered prior to denying a person with a disability benefits, services, and opportunities (28 CFR 35.164 Title II). Postsecondary institutions are obligated to make reasonable accommodations to qualified students with disabilities unless such accommodations cause an undue burden to the institution or fundamentally alter the nature of the program (28 CFR 35.164 [Title II] & 36.302 (a) and 36.303 [Title III]).

The U.S. Department of Education Office for Civil Rights (OCR) recommends that postsecondary institutions develop a plan for the provision of academic adjustments, auxiliary aids and services, and modifications in consultation with the student and person(s) knowledgeable about the disability *(Whittier College of Law [CA]*, 1993). The institution makes no guarantee of a student's academic success *(San Jose State University*, 1993).

Academic adjustment, auxiliary aids, and modifications, together or singly, constitute "reasonable" accommodations. The choice of accommodation is within the discretion of the institution (see Table 4.1). While individual preferences should be respected if possible, the institution may choose an alternative accommodation that is equally effective. All steps necessary must be taken to provide the student with meaningful access to an opportunity to participate. Institutions must demonstrate that consideration was given both to the accommodations requested as well as possible alternatives. Accommodations must be individualized and tailored to meet the student's unique needs. Typically, the student is in the best position to know what accommodations have been successful.

In determining whether an institution of higher education has provided the necessary academic adjustments and auxiliary aids, OCR uses a four-part test whether: (a) the student provided adequate notice that academic adjustments were required; (b) academic adjustments and auxiliary aids were necessary; (c) appropriate academic adjustments and auxiliary aids were provided; and (d) the academic adjustments and auxiliary aids were adequate in terms of quality and effectiveness *(Fort Lewis College [CO]*, 1991; *New York University*, 1992). OCR has consistently ruled against consumers who have failed to request a specific accommodation or failed to inform the institution that the offered accommodation was ineffective.

Table 4.1
Questions to Be Answered in Determining Reasonable Accommodation

- What alternative methods of instruction could be used to present essential programs or course components?

- What auxiliary aids might be beneficial to the student?

- What alternative methods of evaluation could be considered for assessing essential outcome variables and how will these alternative measures be evaluated?

- What are acceptable levels of performance on the alternative measures?

- How will scores from alternative measures be equated with traditional standards?

- Does the student understand the restrictions on accommodating methods of instruction or means of evaluation?

- Can the student meet all essential requirements in spite of his or her disability when given reasonable accomodation?

Note. From "Coming to Terms with the Otherwise Qualified Student with a Learning Disability," by S. S. Scott, 1990, *Journal of Learning Disabilities, 23*, 398-405. Reprinted with permission.

Academic Adjustment

Under Section 504, academic adjustment is considered the modification to the academic requirements that is "necessary to ensure that such requirements do not discriminate or have the effect of discriminating" against a "qualified" applicant or student with a disability (34 CFR 104.44(a)).

Section 504 obligates postsecondary institutions to make necessary modifications and provide auxiliary aids and services unless the accommodations cause an undue burden to the institution or fundamentally alter the nature of the program (*Southeastern Community College v. Davis*, 1979). Modifications may include changes in the length of time permitted for the completion of degree requirements, substitution of specific courses required for completion of degree requirements, and adaptations of the manner in which courses are conducted.

It is important to everyone, disabled or not, that academic and technical standards are maintained. Clarifying for the entire class what objectives must be met to successfully complete a course and course of study will eliminate any perceptions that a student with a disability is being given special favors or a watered-down program. If, despite reasonable accommodation, the student with a disability does not pass an exam and/or maintain a satisfactory GPA, remember that he or she, just as any other student, may simply not have mastered the course material to the degree necessary to pass (*McGregor v. Louisiana State University Board of Supervisors*, 1993; *San Jose State University*, 1993). Students with disabilities have the same right as other students to pass or fail as part of their educational experience. Institutions make no guarantee of a student's academic success.

Test-Taking Accommodations

Extending the time a student takes an examination and altering the manner in which the examination is delivered are examples of academic adjustment. Not all students can be fairly tested under standard administration of regular testing procedures. For example, essay format, oral recitation, multiple choice answer sheets, or laboratory demonstrations for students with visual, hearing, vocal, fine motor, or mobility impairments may require skills irrelevant to the course material being examined (see Table 4.2). An alternative testing method adapted for some students may be a more accurate way to measure ability or achievement (*State University of New York*, 1993).

In order to ensure fairness and equality and to ensure an individual student's ability to function in a testing situation, consistency is one of the most important factors when making this adaptation. This ensures that the modifications do not give students with disabilities a competitive edge, but rather eliminate competitive disadvantage. Academic standards must not be compromised, test results must remain valid and comparable to those of other students in the class.

Changing the test environment, using exam proctors, and extending the time allowed for completion of an exam are appropriate adaptations for many students with a variety of functional limitations. Unless other arrangements are absolutely necessary, students should be allowed to take an adapted test in the same classroom at the same time with the other students. If the adaptation requires the exam to be administered in a place other the regular exam site, efforts should be made to provide a setting that is conducive to concentration. A student should not be expected to cope with taking the exam in a hallway, library main reading room, or department office if telephone, visits, or other distractions will be allowed.

Objective test administration may be best assured by arranging for a proctor other than the student's instructor, reader, or interpreter. Proctors should be trained in ways of reading aloud, writing exactly what is dictated, and maintaining the integrity and ethics of the testing situation. In extending the time for exams, there are no rigid rules for determining how much additional time should be given (see Table 4.3). Extended time should flexibly permit "reasonable progress without dawdling" (Health Resource Center, 1997). *Be flexible with arrangements, but hold a student with a disability to the same academic standards as all other students.*

Table 4.2
Examples of Alternative Testing Procedures*

Impairment	Adaptations
Hearing	Student may be given written instruction on information ordinarily read aloud.
	Oral or sign language interpreter may translate oral instruction and information.
	Interpreter does not interpret the meaning of the written test questions, or supply leading information.
	Where spelling and punctuation are related to course objectives, student and instructor may determine a way for grammar to be evaluated within the parameters of the adaptation.
Vision	Arrangements can be made for special edition of the exam, i.e., on tape, read individually, in larger print, or in braille.
	Student may use electronic or nonoptical aids.
	Student may record answers by typing or taping.
	Student may dictate answers to a proctor, who marks the answer sheet or writes the essay.
Mobility	Arrangements can be made for exam to be given in accessible buildings and classrooms.
	Arrangements can be made for a proctor to assist with manipulation of test materials, marking of exams, and writing of numbers and/or symbols as directed by the student.
	Arrangements can be made for alternative methods of recording answers such as typing or taping.
Speech	Written examinations might be substituted for oral recitation exams.
	Student may write his or her response for an oral recitation and have that presentation read by an interpreter.
	Student may use an auxiliary aid such as a word board or interpreter for classroom participation.
Emotional	Regular exam can be administered individually within the regular time limit.
	Alternative task can be substituted so long as requirements and objectives are suitably met.
Learning disability	Arrangements can be made for alternate methods of recording answers such as typing or taping.
	Test can be given individually in a quiet room without distractions.

Note. From the Health Resource Center, 1997, *Measuring student progress in the classroom. A guide to testing and evaluating progress of students with disabilities.* Reprinted with permission.

Waiving a Course/Examination Requirement

Section 504 regulations require institutions to grant substitution of courses and examinations for the completion of degree requirements (34 CFR, 104.44(a)). However, Section 504 does not require institutions to waive academic requirements deemed essential to the student's program of instruction or to any directly related licensing requirements (*City University of New York*, 1992; *Northern Illinois University*, 1995; *University of Texas at San Antonio*, 1995).

Table 4.3
Factors to Consider in Determining Reasonable Time Extension*

- Type of accommodation

- Exam Format (short answer, multiple choice, open book, essay, paper)

- Experience of the student (prior education or onset of disability)

- Purpose of the course (personal development, career preparation)

Note. From the Health Resource Center, 1997, *Measuring student progress in the classroom. A guide to testing and evaluating progress of students with disabilities.* Reprinted with permission.

Tape Recorders

Institutions of higher education are obligated to permit students with disabilities to use tape recorders in the classroom when a failure to do so will limit the student's opportunity to participate (34 CFR 104.44[b]; *Penn Valley Community College*, 1993).

Auxiliary Aids and Services

There are specific regulations under both Section 504 and the ADA that address the type(s) and provision of auxiliary aids and services (see Table 4.4). Postsecondary institutions must provide auxiliary aids and services for students with impaired sensory, manual, or speaking skills. In determining the necessity of auxiliary aids and services, OCR considers the following: the extent of the disability, the student's prior use of aids, and the nature and relative complexity of the program content *(DeVry Institute of Technology,* 1993*).*

Honoring Communication Choice

Title II of the ADA requires public institutions to give primary consideration to the communication preferences of the individual with a disability unless it can demonstrate that another method is effective (*Petersen v. Hastings Public Schools*, 1994). Title II specifically provides that communications with persons with disabilities must be as effective as communications with others (28 CFR 35.160 (a)). Section 504 also imposes an effectiveness standard for the provision of auxiliary aids and services (*Rochester Institute of Technology*, 1993). Nonetheless, the Department of Justice states that:

a place of public accommodation shall honor the [individual's] choice unless it can be demonstrated that another effective means of communication exists or that use of the means chosen would fundamentally alter the nature of the program or pose an undue burden. (Kincaid, 1995; Tugg v. Tower, 1994)

The issue is not whether the student with a disability is merely provided access, but rather the extent to which communication is actually as effective as that provided to other students.

Fee for Services

Financial considerations do not relieve a recipient of federal funds from its obligations under Section 504 to students whose disabilities require the use of auxiliary aids and services in order to have equal access to educational programs (*College of California*, 1994). The responsibilities of recipients and nonrecipients under ADA are similar to those mandated by Section

504. The ADA and Section 504 make it clear that the institution is ultimately responsible for ensuring auxiliary aids. It is acceptable for an institution to get another source such as a vocational rehabilitation agency to pay for aids and services, but the institution must ensure that the accommodations are present regardless of who pays.

The ADA reinforces OCR's practice that an institution may not charge the student with a disability for the provision of necessary auxiliary aids and services (*Southeast College of Technology*, 1991). Nor is it permissible for the institution to deny necessary services to students who are not low income and, therefore, ineligible to receive vocational rehabilitation assistance (*Camenisch v. University of Texas*, 1980, *vacated as moot*, 1981; *United States v. Board of Trustees of the University of Alabama*, 1990). OCR, however, has ruled that it is permissible to require a student, as a condition of obtaining auxiliary aids, to apply for funds from other sources for which he or she may be eligible (*California Western School of Law*, 1992).

Interpreter Services

As to whether interpreter services are required for students with hearing impairment, OCR cites the Department of Justice in the case involving the *University of California, Davis* (1993) interpretation of the Title II regulations:

> *Although in some circumstances a notepad and written materials may be sufficient to permit effective communication, in other circumstances they may not be sufficient. For example, a qualified interpreter may be necessary when the information being communicated is complex, or is exchanged for a lengthy period of time. Generally, factors to be considered in determining whether an interpreter is required include the context in which the communication is taking place, the number of people involved, and the importance of the communication.*

OCR identified students for whom interpreter services are appropriate as those "for whom auditory assistance or lip reading does not render the classroom accessible." According to Heyward (1995), OCR has

further outlined institutional responsibilities with respect to these students:

> *A hearing impaired (HI) student who enrolls in courses at a postsecondary educational institution is entitled to more than a fellow student paraphrased version of the lecture made available after the class is completed. Even a transcript of the lecture, presented after the class is completed, is not meaningful access for those HI students who are dependent on sign language interpretation for his/her [SIC] interactive communication needs.*

Postsecondary institutions are obligated to provide adequate and qualified interpretation services (*College of the Redwoods*, 1993; 28 CFR 35,105, 28 CFR 36.303; *Great Falls Vocational Technical Center*, 1990). Certified interpreters can handle most interpreting situations while a noncertified interpreter, depending on education and experience, may be capable of interpreting in a college or university environment. Recognizing a national shortage of qualified interpreters, OCR has consistently found colleges and institutions in compliance with ADA/Section 504 who can show that they have made "diligent efforts" to secure such services (*University of California, Davis*, 1993; *University of Massachusetts, Boston*, 1991; *Wentworth Institute of Technology*, 1993).

Real-Time Stenocaptioning

The appropriateness of real-time stenocaptioning must be determined on a case-by-case basis that takes into account the individualized needs of the student with a hearing-impairment, the type of subject matter, and the educational setting involved. "A critical factor in whether steno-interpreting provides meaningful access to the HI student in a ... lecture oriented classroom appears to be the degree of the stenocaptioner's skill" (*University of California, Davis*, 1993).

Notetakers

Although notetakers are not specifically listed as a required auxiliary aid in the Section 504 regulations, they are specifically mentioned as a type of auxiliary aid that may be provided under the ADA (28 CFR 35.104(1) Title I & 28 CFR 36.303(b)(1) Title III). The *purpose* of notetaking — in addition to equal access — is to reduce the time required to review information, which taping does not do. The institution is accountable for the identification of notetakers (*Highline Community College*, 1992). OCR found that there were no violations of Section 504 in giving students options regarding notetakers:

(1) secure their own notetaker; (2) request the professor to make an announcement; or (3) request the Disability Student Services coordinator to secure a notetaker" (New York University, 1992). Institutions are also required to provide students with visual impairment with either the note-taking equipment they need to take their own notes or to ensure that notes will be taken by a classmate in a "directly usable form" (Loyola Marymount University [CA], 1992).

Readers

A qualified reader is an individual who can "clearly convey the information in the reading material" (*City University of New York, Brooklyn, 1996*).

Alternative Formats

Colleges and universities are obligated to provide taped texts and/or printed materials under both Titles II and III of the ADA (28 CFR 35.104.[2] & 28 CFR 36.303[b][2]). Relying too heavily on existing services such as the Recordings for the Blind (RFB) to provide material in an alternative format for students who are blind and for students with learning disabilities, limiting materials and textbooks only to those provided on tape by the library, requiring students to pay RFB membership fees after enrollment, or failing to have a procedure in place for ordering books on tape or in alternative formats in a timely manner are in violation of Section 504 and the ADA (*City University of New York, Brooklyn*, 1996; *San Jose University*, 1993; *State University of New York*, 1993). OCR has ruled that "although

colleges are permitted to use existing resources to provide necessary services, an institution may not refuse to provide auxiliary aids needed by students because it believes that other providers of such services exist. If no other public or private agency is actually available to provide the auxiliary aids, then the institution is required ... to provide such services" (*St. Charles County Community College*, 1991).

Course material in an alternative format must be provided on a timely basis. Institutions must have a system for obtaining translation of required reading materials (textbooks and handouts). "On a timely basis means that actual portions of the reading in the text assigned to the class will be accessible to [the student with visual impairment] and that handouts will be accessible to the [student] when they are distributed to [his or her] classmates" (*Loyola Marymount University* [CA], 1992). Specialized material, such as mathematical symbols and equations, must be translated into a language specifically created to communicate such material to individuals with visual impairments.

Computer Equipment

Recognizing that technological advancements are opening doors to individuals with disabilities, colleges and universities are at a crossroads in ensuring meaningful and equal access to all students. Institutions are responsible for ensuring that on-campus computer systems are accessible to students with disabilities (*Loyola Marymount University* [CA], 1992). In the case of *San Jose State University* (1996), a student with a sight-impairment charged the university with discrimination because it failed to provide equal access to the Internet. It was the opinion of OCR that "if an institution relies on adaptive software to provide access it includes a responsibility to provide the special training necessary to teach the computer user with the disability how to use such software programs." In the case of *City University of New York, Brooklyn* (1996), the University voluntarily agreed to offer training in the use of adaptive computers to students with visual impairments. It also agreed to designate a number of computers for use by students with visual impairments and to provide adaptive equipment or other aids in a timely and effective manner to students with disabilities who require adaptive equipment for computer use. OCR stressed that as technology advances, a college's obligations will change accordingly.

Personal Services

Under both Section 504 and the ADA, institutions are not responsible for the provision of "services of a personal nature." These include personal attendants, individually prescribed devices such as wheelchairs, readers for personal use or study, and personal homework activities such as typing of term papers and use of tutors. Students are liable for their own individual computer hardware and software. However, many colleges and universities have programs that provide these services, such as study skills training, tutoring, and the assignment of learning disabilities specialists who often work one-on-one with students. These services exceed the minimum accommodation required of all institutions to students with disabilities and may be offered for a fee. (If these services are provided free of charge to nondisabled students, however, they must be offered to students with disabilities free of charge.) An institution's responsibility to provide accommodations relates directly to the programs and services it offers. It does not extend to what are in essence collateral needs of the student while he or she happens to be in the postsecondary environment.

Dissatisfaction with Accommodations

As discussed in chapter 5, while an institution should endeavor to provide accommodations that are agreeable to the student, the institution is not required to change accommodations based on the whims of the student. The standard is to provide effective accommodation based upon the identified needs of the student. The student's individual preferences, particularly if they are unreasonable, do not define the nature or the level of services that should be provided.

When faced with a student who continuously disagrees with the services provided, the institution should ask itself whether it has made a good faith effort to provide meaningful access.

The institution should provide written documentation to support decisions that result in students being denied access, opportunities, or benefits. It also would be wise to provide a written record of all accommodation decisions that involved a rejection or modification of the specific requests of individuals, which outlines: (a) why the preferences were rejected or modified and (b) how the accommodations actually provided or offered effectively meet the individual's identified needs.

Contractual Agreements/ Field Placement

The institution is always responsible for students who are participating in its programs whether on or off campus. The question is whether the institution has primary or secondary responsibility. The institution has the ultimate liability for the provision of reasonable accommodation. The intern site generally assumes the duty for providing accommodation on site; the institution, however, must monitor what happens in that environment to ensure that its students are not discriminated against and are provided necessary accommodations (Heyward, 1995) (Also see chapter 5).

Both Section 504 and Title II of the ADA specify that postsecondary institutions, in providing an aid, benefit, or service may not *directly or through contractual arrangements* deny an equal opportunity to students with disabilities on the basis of disability. Postsecondary institutions have an obligation under Section 504 to ensure that other educational programs or activities not operated wholly by them, yet benefiting their students, provide students with disabilities an equal opportunity to participate (Kincaid, 1995).

OCR clearly outlined the responsibilities of institutions in its ruling in a complaint filed against *San Jose State University* (1993). In finding that the intern site personnel failed to provide accommodations and were not adequately prepared or trained to assist the student equaled a violation of the regulations, OCR stated:

Moreover, in this case the University had a responsibility for providing guidance to the county official regarding the provision of academic adjustments or accommodation for students with disabilities. The University's failure to provide such guidance and oversight denied the [student] a meaningful opportunity to participate in violation of 34 CFR 104.4(b)(1)(I). Further, the University violated Section 504, 104.43(b) in turning a part of the student education over to an individual that the University had not adequately prepared or trained to assist the student. This provision required that the University assure itself that the services provided by the county official would allow the [student] equal opportunity to participate in the internship. It is meaningless for an institution to make internship opportunities off campus available to students without ensuring that those internships are, in fact accessible through accommodations to qualified students who require special assistance. It is discriminatory under Section 504 and Title II for the University to have not taken steps to assure that the [student] in this case would receive an opportunity to succeed equal to that of non-disabled students.

Field placement sites cannot just refuse to accept a student with a disability, after disclosure, based on the disability alone. In *Issaqual School District* (1993), OCR found the district in violation of Section 504 and the ADA when the district made a decision not to accept a student with cerebral palsy for a student teaching position without any information that demonstrated that the student, with or without accommodation, would be able to meet any district requirements for student teaching. The acceptance or nonacceptance of a student with a disability should

---

Table 4.4
Applicable Federal Regulations — Section 504 of the Rehabilitation Act

34 CFR 104.44(d)(1) requires an institution to take such steps as are necessary to ensure that an individual with a disability is not denied the opportunity to benefit from or participate in the institution's programs.

34 CFR 104.44(d)(2) defines auxiliary aids and services as including taped texts, interpreters or other methods of making orally delivered material available to students with hearing impairments, readers in libraries for students with visual impairments, classroom equipment adapted for use by students with manual impairments, and other similar services and actions. (See also 28 CFR 35.104 and 28 CFR 36.303.)

Title II ADA

28 CFR 35.105 defines a qualified interpreter as one who is able to interpret effectively, accurately and impartially, both receptively and expressively, using any necessary specialized vocabulary. (See also 28 CFR 36.104 Title III ADA.)

28 CFR 35.160 requires a public institution to give primary consideration to the request of the individual with a disability in determining what types of auxiliary aid and service are necessary.

28 CFR 35.164 provides that a public entity need not take any action that it can demonstrate would result in a fundamental alteration in the nature of a service, program, or activity or would result in a fundamental and administrative burden. If the institution takes the position that the provision of auxiliary aids and services would pose an undue burden or fundamental alteration, the head of the institution or his or her designee must issue a written decision explaining its reasoning, after considering all available resources.

be based on the essential requirements of a student intern in the particular site. Field placement sites should develop standards as well as a procedure for determining acceptable interns that will be used for all students, disabled or not.

Whether to disclose or not disclose a disability to a field placement is a decision of the student. Students with disabilities have the right under ADA (Title II) to be seen first as capable people with marketable skills and only secondarily as people who happen to have disabilities. If the disclosure of their disability is handled inappropriately, the individual with a disability often suffers both positive and negative stereotyping; it raises the level of anxiety of the field placement supervisor and staff, and it evokes a number of behavioral biases on the part of nondisabled people (Rutherford, Merrier, & Parry, 1993).

Under Section 504 and the ADA, field placement coordinators, faculty, and/or institutions do not have the right to disclose a student's disability to any field placement without the written permission of the student (Title I at 42 U.S.C. ss1211[d][3] & [4]; 29 CFR ss1630.14-1630.16). The Family Rights and Privacy Act of 1974 (FERPA), also known as the Buckly Amendment, provides faculty with access to educational information in institutional files regarding students with whom they are working. Disability-related records provided by a physician, psychiatrist, psychologist, or other recognized professional are not subject to free access under FERPA. The Act exempts disability- related records that are used for support of the student and are available only to service providers and other professionals chosen by the student (AHEAD, 1996).

Students with disabilities should be encouraged to disclose their disability as early as possible to the field placement site or to give the field placement coordinator permission, in writing, to disclose after the placement has been made if they desire accommodation(s). A separate disability disclosure form should be used because the general release of information form used by many institutions does not include the release of medical/disability disclosure. The intent of the general release form is only for relevant academic information. The individual with a

disability is already a qualified student and has met the essential standards of the program. Therefore, the decision to disclose or not to disclose is solely the right of the student (see Table 4.5).

Table 4.5
Rules Regarding Confidentiality

- Disability-related information should be treated as medical information and handled under the same strict rules of confidentiality as is other medical information. This includes the comprehensive documentation from an appropriate source that persons with disabilities must provide to establish the existence of their disability and their need for accommodation or consideration.

- Disability-related information should be collected and maintained on separate forms and kept in secure files with limited access.

- Disability-related information should be shared only on a limited basis within the institutional community. It may be shared only when there is a compelling reason for the individual from the institution seeking information regarding some specific aspect of this confidential information.

Note. From the Association of Higher Education and Disability (AHEAD), 1996, *Confidentiality & disability in higher education.* Reprinted with permission.

Academic Accommodation Process

With many aspects of serving students with disabilities remaining blurry, the number of court and agency decision are fleshing out the meaning of Section 504 and the ADA. These decisions should be the guiding forces behind the any academic accommodation process. Two of the most important components of the process are the conveying and receiving of information. Institutions must develop reporting procedures, policies governing the provision of academic adjustments and accommodations, and technical standards and essential requirements. This information must also be communicated to students with disabilities within a timely manner.

An institution cannot wait until a student with disability shows up requesting accommodation to address the issue. Administrators and program directors must take steps early to create a proper compliant environment. Yolanda Brooks, Psy.D, OTR (1996) developed a 10-step process to assist occupational therapy educational programs in integrating the ADA and Section 504 (see Table 4.6).

Furthermore, unilateral decision making regarding the delivery of services should be eliminated. All decisions regarding academic adjustments should adhere to institutional policies and procedures and involve personnel from the disabled student services office and the 504 coordinator. According to Heyward, Lawton, & Associates (1993), by providing strong, visible, and clear support to the disabled student services office, and institution will avoid endless challenges by faculty members regarding the authority of someone who is often viewed as not being part of the academic system. Faculty members must be provided training on policies and procedures, given written guidelines that clearly outline their rights and responsibilities, and be informed about reporting procedures (see Figure 4.1).

Finally, an effective monitoring system should be put into place. All compliance procedures should be monitored on a regular basis to ensure that modifications are made when they are warranted. This also allows for direct and quick action to be taken when violations of policies and procedures are made, including holding individuals accountable who improperly deny accommodations to individuals with disabilities and/or are guilty of discriminatory behavior.

Table 4.6
10-Step Process for Integrating the ADA and Section 504

1. Essential functions
Determine the essential functions of an OT student, including qualifications.

2. Definition of a disability
Provide information on policies and procedures for accommodating students with disabilities. Make sure to make a distinction between disability, impairment, and qualified student based on your definition of essential functions of an OT student.

3. Commitment
Let all within your university, division/school, and program know of your commitment to recruiting, accepting, advancing, and retaining all qualified students, including students with disabilities. Make sure your statement is in concert with the university's general statement. Share this with fieldwork and clinical sites and have copies of their statements and policies on nondiscrimination (keep these in your ADA files).

4. Recruitment
Let it be known in your recruitment efforts that qualified students with disabilities are encouraged to apply.

5. Staff education and training
Train your staff to screen qualified applicants with disabilities. Look at essential functions, the qualifications of the individual, and ways to make reasonable accommodations. Do not allow the individual's disability to distract you as qualifications are evaluated. Be certain any tests or medical exams are performed in accordance to Title I of the ADA. (While this addresses employment, following its guidelines decreases the potential for discriminating against qualified applicants/students.) Follow your guidelines in determining qualifications (including essential functions).

— continued on next page

6. Reasonable accommodations/adaptations

Determine what a reasonable accommodation is and how it would be implemented within your department. Explain the procedures and processes with examples. Make sure to include that these accommodations and adaptations are for students with known disabilities. Be sure to test accommodations and adaptations once the student with disabilities is admitted and the accommodation is determined. Make sure the student has accepted the accommodation and document it. Provide adjustments as necessary, soliciting input from the student, and document actions taken.

7. Education

Any student's success as an OT student hinges on proper education and training. Be sure all educational and training materials, field sites, clinicals, etc., are accessible to your students with disabilities. Coordinate with other departments within the university. Set the example for other departments and make your department available as a resource. Develop and improve your relationship with the university's department of disability services. Remember what OT's do and what value occupational therapy brings to peoples' lives. If people (or sites) you contract/affiliate with discriminate, then you discriminate.

8. Awareness/sensitivity

Explain to staff and students the principle of reasonable accommodations and the particular accommodations that can or have been made.* If the disability is not obvious, disclosure of the disability is not necessary nor is the accommodation. However, informing the students of an accommodation provides important knowledge that can be the key to understanding and accepting. This provides an opportunity to address any myths and misconceptions about people with disabilities, and prevent potential acts of discrimination. Classes and programs on dealing with differences are a critical component for clinicians in training.

(*This disclosure should be made in a general sense, not with a specific student in mind. If you do have a student with an obvious disability, the need for an accommodation is often assumed. However, attitudinal discrimination occurs more frequently when the disability is not obvious, yet it is known that some type of "special treatment" is being provided the student. Disclosing accommodations decreases the likelihood of such misconceptions and allows opportunity for understanding and acceptance. The procedures and processes regarding disclosure of accommodations should be established within the department. In every case, the student needs to have an active role in determining the necessity of disclosure of an accommodation. It should be made clear that disclosure of accommodation is not required, however, the implications of not doing so need to be understood.)

9. Self-evaluation

The self-evaluation for public entities should have been completed within 1 year of January 26, 1992. All entities are encouraged to complete a self-evaluation. Current services, policies, and practices (for both employment and provision of benefits and services) and the effects thereof that do not or may not have met the requirements of the ADA regulations need to be evaluated. It is recommended that an opportunity be provided to interested persons, including individuals with disabilities, to participate in the self-evaluation process. One of the best means to complete a self-evaluation is through a task force committee whose membership reflects the institution and the community it serves. Records and time lines are critical to define areas of strength and need the for changes.

In addition to the requirements mandated for Title II entities, a self-evaluation for OT programs should also include the following:

- information evaluation
- campus evaluation
- building evaluation
- program evaluation
- field site evaluation
- attitudinal evaluation

10. Continuing the process

Ongoing evaluation and adjustments show that occupational therapy sets the standard.

Note. From "Understanding the Americans with Disabilities Act in Occupational Therapy Education Issues for Occupational Therapy Educations," by Y. Brooks, 1996, *ADA and occupational therapy education informational package.* Reprinted with permission.

Postsecondary institutions are faced with the challenge of fulfilling their responsibilities to educate all their students, and students with disabilities are a part of this population. Given the increasing number of students and applicants with a variety of disabling conditions and varying degrees of severity who seek to attend higher education, the process of providing reasonable accommodation is critical to ensuring equal access to educational opportunities. Accommodations academic participation can make a difference in the student's ability to fulfill not only course requirements but also to help fulfill personal goals.

Reasonable accommodation focuses on equalizing opportunities for people with disabilities in education, employment, and access to public services and facilities. Assuring educational access is the responsibility of everyone — the institution, individual programs, faculty, students with disabilities, and nondisabled students. Clearly, there are still many unanswered questions surrounding academic adjustment, auxiliary aids, and services and modifications. There is still a lot work to be done in making colleges and university fully accessible to student with disabilities. Yet, being flexible, creative, and inclusive will pave the way for a truly accessible educational system for all people.

• • •

References

American Association for the Advancement of Science (1991). *Barrier free in brief laboratories and classrooms in science and engineering.* Washington, D.C.

Association on Higher Education and Disability (AHEAD). (1996). *Confidentiality & disability in higher education.* Columbus, OH.

Brooks, Y. (1996). Understanding the Americans with Disabilities Act in occupational therapy education: Issues for occupational therapy educators. *ADA and occupational therapy education informational packet.* Bethesda, MD: American Occupational Therapy Association.

California Western School of Law, Complaint No. 09-92-2004 (OCR Region IX, 1992).

Cambridge Technical Institution (OH), Complaint No. 05-90-2012 (OCR Region V, 1990).

Camenisch v. University of Texas, 616 F.2d 127 (5th Cir.1980) vacated as moot, 451 U.S. 390 (1981).

City University of New York, Brooklyn, Case No. 02-95-2145, (OCR Region II, 1996).

City University of New York, 3 NDLR 104 Complaint No. 02-91-2050 (OCR Region II, 1992).

College of California, 4 NDLR 311 (1994).

College of the Redwoods (CA), Case No. 09-93-2082-I (OCR Region IX, 1993).

DePaul University (IL), 4 NDLR 157, Complaint No. 05-89-2029, (OCR Region V, 1993).

DeVry Institution of Technology, Complaint No. 05-93-2022 (OCR Region V, 1993).

Dixie College, 8 NDLR, 31, Case No. 08-95-2111 (OCR Region VIII, 1995).

Fort Lewis College (CO), Complaint No. 08-91-2023 (OCR Region VIII, 1991).

Great Falls Vocational Technical Center, 1 NDLR 273, Complaint No. 08-90-2029 (OCR Region VIII, 1990).

Health Resource Center. (1997). *Measuring student progress in the classroom: A guide to testing and evaluating progress of students with disabilities.* Washington, DC: American Council on Education.

Heyward, S. (1992). *Access to education for the disabled: A guide to compliance with Section 504 of the Rehabilitation Act of 1973.* Jefferson, NC: McFarland.

Highline Community College (WA), 3 NDLR 151, Complaint No. 10-92-1020 (OCR Region X, 1992).

Issaqual School District, 4 NDLR 72, Complaint NO. 10-93-1031 (OCR Region X, 1993).

Kincaid, J.M. (1994). *A review of case law as applied to students with psychological disabilities in institutions of higher education.* Center Barnstead, NH.

Kincaid, J.M. (1995). *Legal considerations for serving students with learning disabilities in institutions of higher education.* Center Barnstead, NH.

Kincaid, J.M. (1995). *Legal issues specific to serving students who are deaf or hard of hearing in institutions of higher education.* Center Barnstead, NH.

Kincaid, J.M. (1996). *Dancing with wolves: ADA compliance in the 90's.* Center Barnstead, NH: Author.

Loyola Marymount University (CA), Complaint No. 09-91-2157 (OCR Region IX, 1992).

McGregor v. Louisiana State University Board of Supervisors, 4 NDLR 186 3F.3d 850 (5th Cir. 1993).

New York University, 3 NDLR 381, Complaint No. 02-92-2100 (OCR Region II, 1992).

Northern Illinois University, 7 NDLR 392, Case No. 05-95-2082 (OCR Region V, 1995).

Penn Valley Community College (MO), 5 NDLR, 139, Complaint No. 07-93-2026 (OCR Region VII, 1993).

Petersen v. Hastings Public Schools, 4 NDLR 197 (D.NE 1993), *aff'd* 31 F.3d 705, 21 IDELR 377(8th Cir. 1994).

Rochester Institute of Technology, Complaint No. 02-92-2049 (OCR Region II, 1993).

Rutherford, L. Merrier, P., & Parry, L. (Fall 1996). To disclose or not to disclose? *Careers & the Disabled.*

pp. 36–39. Columbus, OH, 1996.

San Jose State University, 4 NDLR 358, Complaint No. 09-93-2161 (OCR Region IX, 1993).

San Jose State University (CA), 4 NDLR 358, Complaint No. 09-93-2034-I (OCR Region IX, 1993).

San Jose University (CA), Complaint No. 09-89-2134 (OCR Region IX, 1990).

Scott, S. (1990). Coming to terms with the otherwise qualified student with a learning disability. *Journal of Learning Disabilities, 23,* 398-405.

Southeast College of Technology, 2 NDLR 36, Complaint No. 04-91-2031 (OCR Region IV, 1991).

Southeastern Community College v. Davis, 442 U.S. 397, 99 S.Ct. 2361 (1979).28 CFR 35.130(b)(7) and 35.164 (Title II); 28 CFR 36.302(a) and 36.303 (Title III).

State University of New York, 4 NDLR 432, Complaint No. 02-93-2088 (OCR Region II, 1993).

St. Charles County Community College, 1 NDLR 348, Complaint No. 07-91-2008 (OCR Region VII, 1991).

St. Thomas University School of Law (FL), Complaint No. 04-94-2093 (OCR Region IV, 1993).

Tugg v. Tower, 5 NDLR 311 (S.D. Fla. 1994).

University of California, Davis, 4 NDLR 108, Complaint No. 09-92-2101-I (OCR Region IX, 1993).

University of California, Santa Barbara, Complaint No. 09-90-2057 (OCR Region IX, 1990).

United States v. Board of Trustees of the University of Alabama, 908 F.2d 740 (11th Cir. 1990).

University of Massachusetts, Boston, Complaint No. 01-90-2067 (OCR Region I, 1991).

University of Texas at San Antonio, 7 NDLR 447, Case No. 06-95-2033 (OCR Region VI, 1995).

Wentworth Institute of Technology (MA), 5 NDLR 190, Complaint No. 01-93-2080 (OCR Region I, 1993).

Western Michigan University, Complaint No. 05-90-2019 (OCR Region V, 1990).

Western Michigan University, 3 NDLR 267 (OCR Region V, 1993).

Whittier College of Law (CA), 4 NDLR 183, Complaint No. 09-93-2048 (OCR Region IX, 1993).

CHAPTER 5

*Educators must recognize the importance of
complying with the procedural considerations ...
and resist the temptation to resort to "knee-jerk"
responses regarding academic freedom and integrity.*

— S. Heyward, 1992

Procedural Considerations

Sally S. Scott

In the preceding chapters, we have reviewed the legal foundations for faculty and colleges to provide access for students with disabilities, examined potential institutional resources and linkages, and discussed process and content in the areas of defining essential requirements and reasonable accommodations within an OT program. In chapter 5, we turn to procedural considerations in implementing policies and nondiscriminatory practices within the OT program. We will discuss issues and provide recommendations for disseminating and using standards and policies, working with individual students, and coordinating efforts between the OT classroom and clinic. We have included a question and answer format at the end of the chapter to address frequent issues that OT faculty face in implementing nondiscriminatory programs.

Dissemination and Use of OT Standards and Policies

Defining essential functions of a course or program of study is a relatively new necessity in higher education. Medical and allied health fields have been some of the most proactive areas in recognizing the importance of this process of clearly conveying standards, at least in part because of the direct and immediate concern for patient safety. Yet, because a recognized core of essential standards does not exist within specific areas such as OT, each program may feel it is on the cutting edge of this process. If the OT program has taken a collaborative approach of soliciting a range of perspectives from various areas of expertise, then the resulting OT standards and policies likely represent multiple perspectives and broad-based consensus. The courts have required that educators make a good faith effort to define essential standards with input from experts knowledgeable about disabilities (*Wynne v. Tufts University School of Medicine*, 1992). Best practice therefore dictates that OT faculty develop essential standards and practices, disseminate this information, and monitor its use to ensure that standards and policies are achieving the desired goal of promoting a nondiscriminatory OT program.

Dissemination of Standards and Policies

After OT essential functions have been defined and policies reviewed, OT faculty must turn to the task of formulating a systematic plan for disseminating this information. In formulating a plan, OT faculty should first investigate current information and outreach efforts on campus. On some campuses, the office for students with disabilities takes an active role in conducting outreach and information dissemination to students and potential students with disabilities. On these campuses, OT faculty should communicate closely with the office for students with disabilities, provide OT-specific information, and coordinate OT efforts with broader institutional outreach efforts. Other campuses may have minimal campus supports and outreach efforts for students with disabilities. On these campuses, OT faculty will need to take a leadership role in disseminating information to potential and current OT students. Regardless of the level of support on campus, OT faculty should consider the education needs of students and OT faculty themselves and devise a plan to disseminate information to these groups.

Student Outreach

In order to convey OT essential standards and policies as clearly and proactively as possible, student education efforts should begin even before matriculation at the college. The admissions department and interviewers at the institution should be provided with essential functions and technical standards of the OT program in order to convey this information to a wide range of prospective students. All publications distributed to prospective students, such as OT program literature or brochures, should contain a statement of nondiscrimination and information on how to contact the office for students with disabilities to request accommodation (see requirements for notification in chapter 3). In addition, these publications should be available in alternative formats.

For students admitted to the institution and/or OT program, orientation materials and activities should also include a brief reference to nondiscriminatory practices and how to request accommodation on campus. If an OT student manual is provided, for example, it should contain a statement of nondiscrimination, contact information for the office for students with disabilities, and a copy of essential requirements to be met with or without accommodation.

Faculty Outreach

Though many OT faculty may be involved in the process of defining essential requirements and OT policies, ongoing education efforts must be made to reach all full- and part-time OT instructors working with students, including new faculty, adjunct faculty, and fieldwork faculty. All faculty need to be informed about federal laws mandating access (Section 504 and the ADA), the faculty role in accommodating qualified students with disabilities, institutional structures and resources, and OT policies and practices for nondiscrimination. The service provider at the office for students with disabilities is often a valuable resource in this education process and may be able to provide general campus literature, speak at new faculty orientation meetings, and provide or coordinate general faculty inservices on disability issues. The office for students with disabilities may offer a faculty handbook that provides specific information about disability characteristics and suggestions for teaching and accommodating students with disabilities.

In addition to these general faculty development efforts, the OT program itself may wish to conduct educational opportunities targeting OT issues. Personnel from the office for students with disabilities could be invited to attend a departmental meeting and address specific questions arising within the OT program. A panel presentation by OT students and clinicians with disabilities can be coordinated to provide a forum for discussion about issues and access within the program and the profession. Another strategy for addressing ongoing faculty education needs is to identify a departmental liaison for disability issues. The liaison should have experienced success in working with students with disabilities, be aware of institutional resources, and be familiar with OT standards and policies. This individual can serve as a contact point for new, adjunct, or clinical faculty with questions about disability access. He or she may be available to discuss OT-specific issues and possible strategies with any OT faculty member who is experiencing difficulties or has questions. In addition, the liaison may serve to promote linkages with the office for students with disabilities. He or she can convey access issues or OT program needs to the office, and communicate new initiatives or opportunities provided by the office for students with disabilities to OT faculty.

Use of Standards and Policies

In the course of defining essential functions and reasonable accommodations, faculty are typically very focused on establishing clear-cut procedures for weighing student qualifications. Proactively discussing and developing policy for essential functions and reasonable accommodations will provide a strong and thoughtful foundation for considering the needs of students with disabilities while maintaining institutional and programmatic integrity. However, there is a potential hazard in viewing essential requirements and technical standards as screening tools and forgetting the spirit of federal laws for individualized equal access. The courts have noted that nondiscriminatory use of essential standards and policies requires a consideration of student need and qualified status on a case-by-case basis (*Davis v. Southeastern Community College*, 1979). It is important for OT faculty to actively monitor the use of essential standards and policies and ensure that they are, in fact, being used to achieve the desired outcome of nondiscrimination for OT students with disabilities. Issues and procedural considerations in applying standards and policies may arise in admissions and in general student treatment within the OT program.

Recruitment and Admission

The first arena in which students will encounter the essential functions and policies of the OT program is in the recruitment and admissions process. Though this process is guided by the *Essentials of an Accredited Occupational Therapy Program,* (AOTA Essentials) requirements vary among programs due to the individual nature of the institution, the OT curricula, and the specific degree or certificate to be awarded. (See Chapter 3 for a discussion of developing technical standards and essential requirements that reflect a particular program and level of training.) The actual process of recruitment and admission also varies among institutions from being a process solely managed by the admissions department, to one that is managed by the OT department, to a process that involves the participation of OT faculty and admissions staff.

Whatever admissions procedures are used on a campus, it is vital to consider several important principles in promoting nondiscriminatory admissions practices to the institution or OT program itself (see Table 5.1). These principles are interrelated and, in application, will likely overlap. But each principle has been gleaned from case law as necessary in nondiscriminatory admissions considerations. OT faculty may wish to use these principles to monitor the effectiveness of the OT essential academic and technical standards and ensure that they are being applied in a nondiscriminatory way.

Table 5.1
Important Principles in Weighing Admissions Decisions

- Categorical exclusions based on disability label are discriminatory.

- Applicants must be evaluated on the basis of their individual skills and abilities.

- Individuals with disabilities are entitled to the same opportunities to succeed or fail in a program as nondisabled individuals.

- Admissions decisions must include consideration of reasonable accommodations that would permit the individual to participate in the program.

- All criteria used must be legitimate, rationally related to the program's stated purpose, and applied in a nondiscriminatory way.

Categorical exclusions based on a disability label are discriminatory. The mere presence of a disability is not sufficient grounds for assuming that a student will not be able to function in a given OT program (*Kling v. County of Los Angeles*, 1985; *Pushkin v. Regents of the University of Colorado*, 1981). For example, all students with hearing impairments should not automatically be denied admission to the OT program because they might have trouble communicating with patients. As clarified in subsequent principles, the abilities and qualifications of individuals must be considered on a case-by-case basis. Heyward, Lawton, and Associates (1993) cautioned that the danger of "listing particular skills and abilities as admission criteria is that it invariably leads decisionmakers to focus on disabilities in general as opposed to individuals in particular."

Applicants must be evaluated on the basis of their individual skills and abilities. As discussed in Chapter 1, federal law protects individuals with a wide range of disabilities from discrimination. Within each disability label, however, there is extensive variability in the severity of the disability and actual functional impact on the individual's performance in a specific setting. For example, the accommodation needs of individuals with visual impairments may range from the use of glasses, to the use of large print, to the use of a guide dog. Institutions are not required to disregard the functional impact of the disability, but may not make general assumptions about functional limitations. Rather, the institution must consider the strengths and abilities an individual brings to the specific context that may enable meeting essential requirements *(Davis v. Southeastern Community College, 1979; School Board of Nassau County v. Arline, 1987).*

Individuals with disabilities are entitled to the same opportunities to succeed or fail in a program as nondisabled individuals. If a student meets admission standards, he or she must be given the opportunity to attempt the program, just as any other student would be. It is discriminatory to deny access to an individual with a disability because he or she *might not* be able to function in a specific situation or the accommodation *might not* allow the student to succeed. For example, in *Pushkin v. Regents of the University or Colorado* (1981) an applicant with multiple sclerosis was denied access to the psychiatric residency program because, though he met academic admission requirements, faculty interviewers felt the individual's physical condition might be difficult for patients to accept and that the applicant had unresolved emotional problems

regarding his illness. The court found these assumptions to be subjective and based on disability stereotypes rather than the specific evidence pertaining to the qualifications of the individual. Providing equal opportunities for qualified applicants to participate in the OT program, however, equally obligates the student to meet program expectations once admitted. As with any other student, admission to the program does not guarantee success. If the student is provided reasonable accommodation based on individual needs, but does not meet program expectations and requirements, it is not considered discriminatory to fail the student. The student must merely be provided the same opportunity to succeed or fail in the OT program as are all other students.

Admissions decisions must include consideration of reasonable accommodations that would permit the individual to participate in the program (Davis v. Southeastern Community College, 1979). The ADA clarified that an otherwise qualified person with a disability is one who can meet the essential requirements of a program with or without accommodation. As discussed in Chapter 4, a range of potential accommodations exists for consideration on an individualized basis. Determining which accommodations are reasonable has been discussed in depth in Chapter 4, but by definition of reasonable, these accommodations do not fundamentally alter or compromise the essential nature of the institution or OT program. For example, a student with a learning disability might, depending on individual documented need, be entitled to extended time in taking the SATs or other standardized entrance examinations. Extended time would be deemed a reasonable accommodation. The institution may not devalue the test scores because the test was taken under nonstandard administration *(SUNY Health Science Center at Brooklyn, 1993).*

All criteria used must be legitimate, rationally related to the program's stated purpose, and applied in a nondiscriminatory way (Davis v. Southeastern Community College, 1979). Criteria that are legitimate and rationally related to the program's purpose are likely outcomes of the process and considerations for developing standards described in detail in Chapter 3.

These essential standards must then must be applied to all applicants with or without disabilities. Essential requirements are not to be used as additional or more stringent criteria applied exclusively to individuals with disabilities *(Coleman v. Zatechka, 1993)*, but rather should provide guidance on requirements for all students.

General OT Student Treatment

In addition to being aware of these important principles in the use of essential requirements in the admissions process, OT faculty should monitor the general accessibility of the OT program for OT students with disabilities. In the preceding chapters, we have emphasized developing objective criteria and considering individual student requests on a case-by-case basis. In addition to responding to individual student needs in specific contexts, it is important to examine the accessibility of the OT program as a whole and assess overall student experiences. The best source of such information will be the students with disabilities themselves.

The letter of the law in Section 504 and the ADA mandates that colleges not discriminate. The spirit of these laws, however, is intended to ensure equal access for individuals with disabilities. Discrimination can take on many forms and degrees ranging from overt to quite subtle. In a survey of college students with disabilities in Virginia, 86% reported encountering barriers to college access (West, Kregel, Getzel, Zhu, Ipsen & Martin, 1993). Discrimination was experienced in physical, programmatic, and attitudinal arenas. Of those barriers, physical access is perhaps the easiest obstacle to conceptualize and identify.

The preceding chapters of this book have largely focused on preventing programmatic discrimination. Attitudinal barriers to access can be difficult to identify, and likely pose the greatest risk to student access and success in the OT program. It is recommended that OT faculty incorporate a mechanism for student feedback within the program in order to detect overt and subtle barriers students may be experiencing. Again, depending on the level of disability support at

an institution, the OSD may be able to assist in this process. Student feedback could be obtained through a voluntary focus group discussion, a student survey, or follow-up with graduates with disabilities. The general purpose of such measures is to ascertain overall student experience in the OT program and to examine accessibility from a broader perspective than merely providing required accommodations. Students may identify areas or policies that need to be revised as well as provide suggestions for improving physical, programmatic, or attitudinal access.

Working with Individual Students

In addition to considering nondiscriminatory practices for the OT program in general, it is important that individual OT faculty are familiar with "best practices" in interacting with individual students with disabilities. These interactions are often at the heart of a nondiscriminatory college program. We will examine procedural considerations in a number of areas pertaining to daily interactions between faculty and individual students, identify potential issues, and provide recommended strategies. In Chapter 6, we will go beyond procedural requirements and provide recommendations for enhancing student empowerment.

Students Who Self-Identify

Some students will identify themselves as having a disability directly to individual faculty and request accommodation. It is important at this point that all classroom and clinical OT faculty are aware of institutional channels and procedures for requesting accommodation and require students to follow these procedures. As described in Chapter 2, the office for students with disabilities typically requires students to register with the office before receiving accommodations. If this is the policy at an institution, regardless of the validity of the accommodation request, OT faculty should refer students to and require that they register with the office for students with disabilities before providing accommodation. Potential issues may arise if the student has not followed institutional procedures by registering with the office for students with disabilities. For example, a student may request an accommodation that exceeds individual needs. It is the role of the OSD to review confidential disability documentation and provide recommendations for appropriate accommodation. Conversely, a student with a disability may feel that an accommodation, though well intentioned, was not provided in a satisfactory way. It is the dual role of the office for students with disabilities to provide assistance in how accommodations are delivered and to monitor student and faculty rights.

When a student self-identifies and requests accommodation, clinical and classroom OT faculty then should inform the student that they will provide needed accommodations when they have received confirmation that the student is registered with the office for students with disabilities and that the specific accommodation has been recommended by that office as appropriate for the individual student. Confirmation of registration and accommodation is typically provided by a confidential letter from the OSD.

Students with Suspected Disabilities

OT faculty, due to their educational background and clinical experience, may recognize some students who are experiencing difficulties and seem to have characteristics indicative of a disability. The characteristics typically indicate one of the invisible disabilities, such as a learning disability or attention deficit. It may be that the student appears to understand course concepts and contributes well to class discussion but fails written tests. Or perhaps the student does well in academic concepts but is surprisingly incompetent in the clinical component of the program. When the student demonstrates potential to do well in the OT program, is not performing up to expectations, and has characteristics of a disability, a number of possible issues arise. For example, a student who has a disability that has not been diagnosed may fail unnecessarily because of the absence of needed accommodations.

On the other hand, the student may be aware of the disability and choose not to self-disclose. Many students

with invisible disabilities try to leave these disabilities labels behind once they graduate from high school. They sometimes fear that faculty and others will not understand the disability and consider them less capable. In these cases, faculty must respect the student's right to confidentiality and to not request accommodation. The consequences of such a choice are, of course, the student's responsibility.

So what should faculty do when they suspect a student may have a disability, but the student has not identified the issue to the faculty member? Well, certainly not all students who are having academic difficulties have a disability. There are many possible reasons that students do not always perform up to expectations. If a faculty member does suspect a disability may be causing academic difficulties, the first step is to discuss the situation with the student. The discussion should focus on the student's performance in a situation. Faculty should avoid the role of diagnostician. The faculty member might initiate the conversation during a private appointment with the student by describing exactly what has been observed in the student's performance and asking the student if he or she has any explanation of why difficulties are occurring. At this point, the student may: (1) offer an explanation unrelated to disabilities; (2) explain that he or she had a disability diagnosed in the past; or (3) not know why he or she is experiencing academic difficulties. If the student reveals that a disability was diagnosed in the past, the student should be referred to the office for students with disabilities. Some students may not be aware that accommodations are a legitimate part of access to higher education and that support is available. If the student is unsure of why he or she is not performing well, it may be that the faculty member has detected an undiagnosed disability. (See examples of faculty observations revealing undiagnosed disabilities in Table 5.2.)

Many college students with learning disabilities, for example, are extremely bright and have managed to perform well throughout high school because of well-developed compensation strategies. When these students enter college, the academic demands are greatly increased and often the familiar compensation strategies that worked in the past are not sufficient to meet the demands of a college setting. Such students may discover for the first time at the college level that they have a learning disability. McGuire, Litt, and Ramirez (1993), for example, noted that 23% of students with learning disabilities registering for support services at the University of Connecticut were diagnosed with learning disabilities for the first time at the university level. OT faculty should refer such students to the office for students with disabilities for screening for a possible disability. Often the service provider can ascertain whether the student needs further more formalized testing, or whether the student would benefit from other supports on campus such as peer tutoring or training on how to improve study skills.

Processing Accommodation Requests

After students have registered with the office for students with disabilities and self-identified to an OT faculty member, students will typically request an accommodation. Chapter 4 discussed in depth the process of weighing reasonable accommodations. The majority of the time, such accommodation decisions are fairly straightforward and easy to address. There are times, however, when individual situations are more difficult and procedural considerations become important for OT faculty in agreeing upon and providing reasonable accommodations.

Student Responsibilities

As discussed in chapter 1, students have specific rights and responsibilities under federal law in attaining equal access to higher education. In order to obtain accommodations from OT faculty, students with disabilities have the responsibility to follow any institutional procedures that have been put in place for requesting specific accommodations. This typically includes registering with the support office and providing adequate documentation of the disability and related needs. OT faculty may legitimately refuse to provide accommodations until the student has complied with such procedures. Sometimes OT faculty may

---

Table 5.2
Examples of Faculty Observations Revealing Undiagnosed Disabilities

Faculty Observation	Later Diagnosis
• Student demonstrated mild clumsiness while administering standardized evaluation tools	Multiple sclerosis
• Student demonstrated difficulties following verbal directions only in situations where background noise was present.	Progressive hearing loss
• Student demonstrated poor written performance on timed tests, delayed reaction time in responding to questions that required recall of dates, events, situations within the past week, yet no problem with immediate recall or longer term recall of the same information.	Head trauma in adolescence

Note. From *Ethnographic Record Reviews.* Submitted by Kimberly Hartmann, OTR, Program Director, Quinnipiac College, 1987-1997. Printed with permission.

be asked by the OSD to provide an accommodation on a limited interim basis while the student attains needed documentation.

Faculty Responsibilities

It is becoming more and more difficult to provide uniform classroom instruction due to the ever-increasing number of students with disabilities who are entering postsecondary institutions. The increasing complexity of accommodation requests is bringing the academic integrity of educational programs into question, while the input of faculty is being solicited less and less. Therefore the rights and responsibilities of the faculty should be clearly communicated and delineated (see Table 5.3).

Table 5.3
Faculty Member Responsibility

- Ensure that students with disabilities request services and accommodations according to the institution's procedures and/or 504 coordinator and/or disabled student services office.

- Make requested academic adjustments and/or modifications that provide equal educational access to qualified students with disabilities.

- Challenge accommodation requests if: (1) the accommodation will alter the fundamental nature of the program/course, (2) the accommodation imposes an undue financial burden and/or hardship on the institution, or (3) the student is not qualified.

- Work in collaboration with the service provider (504 coordinator/disabled student service) and student to resolve any conflicts.

Faculty members are not independent contractors. They must accept that by being employees of an institution that has compliance responsibilities under federal statutes and regulations, they also have a responsibility to assist the institution in satisfying its compliance obligations. There is a shared responsibility between the institution and the faculty in the provision of academic adjustment and reasonable accommodation for those qualified students with disabilities. There have been several judicial decisions in which persons who have improperly denied services, benefits, and opportunities to individuals with disabilities have been held personally liable for those discriminatory acts. *Howe v. Hull* 1994 states that

> *An individual may be subject to personal liability under the ADA. Given the broad language and remedial purposes of the ADA, allowing individual liability in certain circumstances ... is consistent with both the plain language of the statute and congressional intent. To hold differently would allow individuals with both the authority and the discretion to make decisions based on a discriminatory animus to violate the ADA with a degree of impunity not envisioned by Congress.*

The court outlined the circumstances under which an individual may be held personally liable as being:

> *... where (a) he or she is in a position of authority; (b) within the ambit of authority he or she has both the power and discretion to perform potentially discriminatory acts; and (c) the discriminatory acts are the result of the exercise of the individual's own discretion, as opposed to the implementation of institutional policy or the mandates of superiors. (U.S. v. Morant; 1994)*

Faculty members who insist upon taking unilateral action and/or placing themselves directly at odds with institutional policies and mandates regarding the delivery of services to students with disabilities may risk being held personally liable for any resulting violations of federal statutes and regulations.

Faculty members are responsible for ensuring that students with disabilities who provide information to them and/or request services are referred to the appropriate office or procedure that has been established by the institution for obtaining accommodation. It is not the responsibility of faculty members to determine the type(s) of accommodations or modifications for students with disabilities, even if the student contacts them directly. With the rising number of cases in which students are asserting that faculty members are denying them accommodations, institutions should develop regular reporting procedures for their faculty to ensure that the appropriate officials are informed of requests being made directly to the faculty members. This would protect the institution and the individual faculty member from being held responsible for a unilateral decision as well as impress upon all faculty members the importance of involving all necessary parties in accommodation decisions.

Faculty members are required to make all modifications that have been requested through the proper procedures, that essentially provide equal access to students with disabilities (Table 5.4).

Table 5.4
General Guidelines for Faculty Members in the Classroom

- Maintain student confidentiality. Do not singly discuss issues in front of class or other students.

- Treat the student with a disability as you would any other student, recognizing the need for adjustments in classroom practices (e.g., verbalizing overhead projection information for visually impaired students).

- Ask the student if he or she needs help but refrain from insisting if declined. Students vary in the extent to which they are assertive in requesting assistance and in the degree to which it is desired.

- Maintain the same standards for all students but be flexible in determining how those standards are reached; tailor requirements to individual abilities.

- Consider alternative assignments as a substitution for course requirements where appropriate.

- Ensure that critical information about the course requirements, deadlines, scheduling, and tests is conveyed in an accessible format.

Note. From Allegany Community College, *Teaching students with disabilities: Faculty guidebook.* Reprinted with permission.

Changes in the length of time permitted for the completion of degree requirements, substitution of specific course requirements, and adaptation of the manner in which specific courses are conducted are examples of acceptable modifications. Faculty members, however, are not required to make modifications that alter the nature and context of what they are teaching. They are also not required to provide accommodations that have an adverse impact on the integrity of the academic program (Table 5.5).

Denial of Accommodations

Colleges and universities must be able to provide adequate justification and detailed written documentation for all decisions that result in the denial of services, opportunities, and benefits to students with disabilities. According to Heyward (1995), there are numerous judicial decisions in which courts have held that the opinions of individuals who are not knowledgeable will not be accepted as support for decisions that have an adverse impact on individuals with disabilities. For example, if a student provides documentation from an expert in the field that establishes that he or she has a learning disability, the opinion of faculty members who have no expertise in the field of learning disabilities and who question the diagnosis is not sufficient to support a determination that the student is not entitled to accommodations.

In *DePaul University (IL), 1993,* OCR ruled that a committee's decision to deny a student readmission violated the regulations implementing Section 504 because: "The Readmission Committee members received no training in how to handle a petition which raised a handicapping condition. The committee received no special instructions regarding how to consider the [student's] handicap and the extent to which she had been able to demonstrate her ability to succeed in the program prior to her dismissal. Furthermore, no member of the committee spoke to any experts in the field ... "

Table 5.5
General Accommodations in the Classroom — Teaching Methods

The way a class is taught matters to all students including students with disabilities. Here are some basic lecture and discussion techniques that are likely to help

- Speak clearly. Write legibly. This will help all students including students who are hearing or visually impaired.

- Read out loud what you write on the blackboard. This technique will help a student who may be taping the lecture.

- Avoid standing with your back to a window or other source of light. Students who are deaf or hard of hearing look to a well-lit face for important communication cues.

- Use visual aids whenever needed. Describe the visual aid for the student who is visually impaired. This will also make the material more memorable for those who can see.

General accommodations in the laboratory

There are several ways a professor or instructor can help a student with a disability in the laboratory:

- Use of lab partners is very helpful. The lab instructor can help by making sure everyone has a congenial partner or group and has the opportunity to participate fully.

- Use of assistive technology such as light-level indicators, lever controls, or voice output devices may eliminate or reduce the need for lab assistants.

- Check occasionally to make sure the arrangements you and the students have made are working well, and make adjustments if necessary.

- If a student needs more time to complete the lab, he or she may be permitted to enter another lab section.

Student with disabilities are not a safety risk

- Have a visual alarm for students who are deaf or hard-of-hearing.

- Give the student with a visual impairment the chance to become familiar with the lab environment before the first session. Make should the student is given an individual orientation and shown the location of exits and extinguishers.

Accommodations for students with hearing impairments

- Make sure that students have optimal seating arrangements. If a student uses an interpreter, the student should be able to see both you and the interpreter.

— continued on next page

- Face the student when you speak, and keep your face visible and well lit. Speak clearly but naturally.

- Whenever possible use captioned films or videos.

- Speak to the student and not the interpreter.

- Make sure the student has arranged for a notetaker. Insert appropriate pauses during demonstrations. A student cannot lipread or use an interpreter at the same time that he or she is taking notes, watching a demonstration, or reading written material.

- At the beginning of a session or after an interval of silence, draw the student's attention before speaking. This can be done making eye contact, tapping gently on the shoulder, or using some other method worked out with the student. When calling on a student who is hearing impaired make sure you establish eye contact first.

Accommodations for students who are visually impaired

- Provide reading lists or syllabi in advance so that arrangements can be made to transcribe texts to tape or braille.

- Call on students who are blind by name.

- Read out loud whatever you write on the blackboard. To the extent practical, explain in words visual aids or cues you use. Spell difficult or unusual words.

- Copies of your lecture notes may be useful to a visually impaired student with an enlarger.

Accommodations for students who have mobility impairments

- Make sure that the classroom/laboratory is accessible to people who use wheelchairs.

- Recognize that handwriting may be difficult for many students with mobility impairments. Allow the student to use a tape recorder or make sure the student has arranged for a notetaker, if necessary.

- Make sure students with mobility-impairments are not relegated to a doorway, a side aisle, or the back of the room.

- Aisle widths of 42 to 48 inches will allow a wheelchair to maneuver easily.

- Work surfaces should be no higher than 30 inches from the floor. Cleared spaces under the work surfaces should be 29 inches high, 36 inches wide, and at least 20 inches deep to allow leg space for someone seated in a wheelchair.

Note. From the American Association for the Advancement of Science, 1991, *Barrier-free in brief, laboratories and classrooms in science and engineering.* Reprinted with permission.

Titles II and III of the ADA, which regulate public and private institutions, specifically refer to the right of an institution to exclude an individual from participation in its programs, services, or activities for health and safety reasons (28 CFR 36.208 [direct threat]; Kincaid, 1994). Unlike the employment provisions of Title I, an institution may only deny participation to a student with a disability when the student's behavior endangers the health or safety of others *(Cambridge Technical Institution, 1990; Western Michigan University, 1993).*

In the case of *Western Michigan University (1990),* the university was not in violation of Section 504 and the ADA when it dismissed a student with a mental disability because she was unable to participate effectively in the university's educational program. The student had made frequent outbursts and disruptions during class; the student was observed in her dormitory to be in a "psychotic" state; and the director of counseling met with the student and found her to be incoherent. OCR stated:

> *The Director of Counseling's evaluation of the complainant's mental condition and ability to perform effectively as a student are substantially matters of professional judgment. The principal's objections to the complainant's remaining at the University without some form of treatment clearly involved his expertise as a psychologist. OCR will not substitute its judgement for that of an individual clearly qualified to determine whether the complainant should remain at the university without treatment.*

OCR upheld a college dismissal of a student who stalked and harassed a professor although there was no evidence that the student had a mental impairment.

Legitimate Objections

When a student with a disability registers for services and requests an accommodation, it is exactly that — a request. Though the faculty member may not discriminate against the student, he or she can participate in a discussion of what is a reasonable accommodation for a particular student in his or her class. This does not provide the faculty member

with the option to refuse to accommodate students with disabilities. In fact, faculty who have tried to exercise that option have been held personally liable for violating federal law *(Dinsmore v. Pugh and the Regents of the University of California,* 1989, as cited in Heyward, Lawton, and Associates, 1992). But it does permit faculty to provide input as to what constitutes a reasonable accommodation in individual circumstances and contexts. As a starting point, this negotiation typically involves the student with a disability, the campus service provider, and the faculty member. Heyward, Lawton, and Associates (1995a) noted the following areas as legitimate objections to specific accommodation requests: (1) the student does not meet prerequisite requirements or standards; (2) the accommodation would result in a fundamental alteration of the course or program; (3) the accommodation is of a personal nature; or (4) the accommodation would impose an undue financial or administrative burden.

Faculty members who wish to object to the accommodation request of a student must ensure that their objections are legitimate. Those wishing to challenge accommodation requests must establish that:

> *specific skills and abilities of the particular student were taken into account; the identified factor does in fact reflect legitimate concerns regarding the particular situation; and a good faith effort was made to protect access to the student*

(Heyward, Lawton, and Associates, 1993). While the accommodation request is being challenged, the faculty member is still required to provide the requested accommodation (see Table 5.6). Legitimate objections should be raised in a negotiation of accommodation requests and based on individual abilities, needs, and the specific context. A good faith effort should still be made to agree upon a means of providing access for the student. If an accommodation request is rejected or modified, OT faculty might be prudent to keep written documentation that outlines why the accommodation request was rejected or modified and how the alternate accommodation effectively meets the student's individual needs (Heyward, Lawton, and Associates,

1995b). When resolution cannot be reached, campuses are required to have a grievance process to resolve such disputes in a timely manner.

The institution is legally responsible for the action of a faculty member who violates Section 504 or the ADA by refusing to provide a legitimate request for accommodations. Institutions should foster conditions that will create a positive, productive compliance environment for interactions among faculty members, service providers (504 coordinator/OSD), and students. All participants should be committed to resolutions that properly balance legitimate academic concerns and the responsibility to provide educational access to students with disabilities.

Coordinating Efforts Between the OT Department and the Clinical Site

As described in chapter 1, students with disabilities are entitled to access to the full range of programs and activities offered by the college. As a required part of the OT program, fieldwork must also be accessible to students with disabilities under the same nondiscriminatory standards held by the college. The clinical requirement is deemed an integral part of the education program regardless of the fact that a third party offers the education site. Coordinating efforts to educate students with disabilities may give rise to procedural issues in promoting the accessibility of clinical sites and in working with individual students across sites.

Promoting Clinical Site Accessibility

When viewed in its entirety, the OT program must offer OT students with disabilities the same range and quality of choice in clinical sites as other OT students. When students are assigned to fieldwork, students with disabilities must be provided access and necessary accommodations at those sites. The clinical site generally assumes responsibility for providing accommodation onsite (Heyward, Lawton, & Associates, 1995b), but the institution must monitor the

student experience in order to ensure that OT students are not discriminated against and receive needed accommodations.

Currently, in the U.S. health care arena, we are facing many challenges to training students in the field. These issues include: a shortage of fieldwork sites, increasing liability costs to train students, constraints within a managed care system, shortage of therapists qualified to supervise students, increased need for billable hours and thus less free time to train students, and the increased number of OT programs that are requesting fieldwork training sites. These clinical issues may add to the concerns of a fieldwork site when the supervisors are faced with the perceived additional challenge of supervising a student with a disability. However, via collaboration among the clinical site, the institution, and the student a valuable experience for all persons can be created.

Working with Students Across Sites: Frequent Questions

1. *If I think an accommodation is unreasonable, what should I do?*

When a student registers with the office for students with disabilities, he or she will typically go over diagnostic information with the service provider and generate a list of possible accommodations that may be appropriate. These accommodations are considered a "generic" list that must be assessed for each class the student takes to determine whether the accommodation is reasonable and will not compromise essential requirements in that specific context. If a student requests an accommodation that you feel compromises the essential standards in your class, you should discuss alternative accommodations with the student and/or disability service provider that will ensure access for the student. Accommodation is required, but the faculty member is entitled to input as to what form the accommodation will take if the accommodation threatens to change the essential requirements of the course.

2. Who is responsible for paying for student accommodations?

Students with disabilities must be provided with equal access to the institution and its educational programs at no cost to the student. This includes all services, accommodations, or programmatic adjustments that are necessary for the student to have an equal opportunity to participate in the educational experience. Federal regulations do not specify that the services must be paid for by the institution, only that the institution is responsible for seeing that those services are in place in a timely fashion at no cost to the student. Many institutions work collaboratively with vocational rehabilitation, other state agencies, or community service organizations to help alleviate expenses.

3. Can the college note that accommodation has been made on the student's transcript?

The answer to this question depends on the documentation practices of the individual institution. If the college notes all coursework accommodations or alterations on the transcripts of *all students*, then it is not discriminatory to also note these accommodations on the transcripts of students with disabilities. It would be considered discriminatory, however, to only document the accommodations provided for students with disabilities or to document these accommodations more thoroughly than with other nondisabled students. Noting such accommodations as extended time or testing in a separate room only on the transcripts of students with disabilities would constitute differential treatment on the basis of disability and thus be considered discriminatory.

4. How much time is appropriate for extended time?

Extended time, like all reasonable accommodations, must be determined by the needs of the individual student. OT faculty should consult with their campus office for students with disabilities (OSD) for a specific recommendation for individual students based on confidential disability documentation. Typically, it is recommended that students receive an additional 50% of time allocated for other students on the exam. (Extended time for a 1-hour exam is often 1 1/2 hours, a 2-hour exam would be extended to 3 hours, and so forth.) However, there are several variables that guide the determination of a "reasonable" amount of time for a specific individual. The OSD will consider the type of disability and how the student's disability will likely interact with the format of the test (e.g., multiple choice, essay, scantron, etc.). The OSD may consider whether other accommodations (such as the use of a scribe) may increase time requirements. The OSD may review high school records or accommodations to see what has worked in the past for the individual student.

5. How do I know if an accommodation is working?

Determining the effectiveness of an accommodation is the responsibility of the student with a disability. If the student feels the accommodation is not allowing equal access, other accommodations may need to be tried in an effort to best match individual student disability-related needs and the demands of the specific class or clinical setting. It is important for OT faculty to remember that student outcomes are not a reliable source of determining the appropriateness of the accommodation. If the student receives a reasonable accommodation and acquires the best exam score in the class, it doesn't mean that the student has been overaccommodated. Conversely, if the student has received a reasonable accommodation and fails the exam, it doesn't mean the student was discriminated against.

6. Can an accommodation deemed reasonable in a classroom or lab setting be denied the student in a fieldwork situation?

Reasonable accommodations are based on individual disability-related needs in specific contexts. Just because a student has received an accommodation in one setting, it does not necessarily follow that same accommodation will be reasonable in all contexts. If this situation arises, we recommend that the student, the fieldwork site educator, and the academic clinical coordinator meet to review the essentials of the fieldwork training program that cannot be compromised, discuss possible accommodations, and develop a plan that addresses the student's specific access needs. Once again, the intent of such a plan is not to guarantee success, but to create an equal opportunity to participate in the fieldwork experience. As in all clinical situations, the client's safety and health must not be jeopardized. The process of this discussion and accommodation plan should be documented in order to demonstrate a good faith effort in meeting the student's access needs. If agreement on an accommodation cannot be reached, the student should initiate a grievance procedure.

7. May the OT program allow a student with a disability extended time to complete the given degree or certificate even if the catalog and AOTA Essentials state time parameters for program completion?

Once again, reflection upon the essential requirements of the program is necessary. We do not wish to compromise standards of the program nor of the profession. We also have an ethical obligation to society and our clients to ensure that OT graduates meet essential standards. However, the utilization of some accommodations may necessitate extended time in a variety of ways and, therefore, in specific situations it may be reasonable that completion of the essentials of the program and degree requirements may take longer. We suggest that you discuss this issue with your on-campus OSD and possibly the institution's legal counsel.

• • •

References

Allegany Community College. *Teaching students with disabilities: Faculty guide book.* Cumberland, MD: Instructional Assistance Center.

Big Bend Community College (WA), Complaint No. 10-90-2035 (OCR Region X, 1991).

Coleman v. Zatechka, 824 F. Supp. 1360, D. Nev., 1993.

Davis v. Southeastern Community College, 442 U.S. 397, 99 S. Ct. 2361, 60L. Ed. 2D 980, 1979.

Dinsmore v. Pugh and the Regents of the University of California at Berkeley, settled 1989. Heyward, Lawton, & Associates. (1991). Provision of academic accommodations. *Disability Accommodation Digest,* 1 (1), 1, 4. 50 U.S.L.W. 2366.

Heyward, S. (1992). *Access to education for the disabled: A guide to compliance with Section 504 of the Rehabilitation Act of 1973.* Jefferson, NC: McFarland.

Heyward, S. (1995, Oct. 18). Videoconference: Support services for students with disabilities in postsecondary education settings. Sponsored by The Rehabilitation Research and Training Center on Blindness and Low Vision, Department of Counselor Education and Educational Psychology, Division of Continuing Education and the University Television Center, live via satellite from the Mississippi State University.

Heyward, Lawton & Associates. (1993). Faculty members and service providers: The unhappy alliance. *Disability Accommodation Digest.*

Heyward, Lawton & Associates. (Eds). (1993). Medical school admissions. *Disability Accommodations Digest, 3*(3), 3.

Heyward, Lawton & Associates. (Eds.). (1995a). Faculty members and service providers: The unhappy alliance. *Disability Accommodation Digest, 4*(3 , 4), 3.

Heyward, Lawton & Associates. (Eds.). (1995b). Readers' Digest: A special "ask the expert." *Disability Accommodation Digest*, 5(2), 1–7.

Howe v. Hull, 873 F. Supp. 72 77 (N.D. Ohio 1994).

Kling v. County of Los Angeles 769F 2d 532 (9th Cir.), 1985.

McGuire, J., Litt, A., and Ramirez, M. (October, 1993). *A follow-up investigation of the instructional needs of college students with learning disabilities.* Paper presented at the 15th International Conference of the Council for Learning Disabilities, Baltimore, MD.

Pushkin v. Regents of the University of Colorado 685 F. 2D 1372 (10th Cir.),1981.

Rancho Santiago Community College (CA), 3 NDLR 52, Complaint No. 09-92-2049 (OCR Region IX, 1992).

School Board of Nassau County v. Arline, 107 U.S. 1123, 1987.

Simon, S. (1995, Oct. 18). Videoconference: Support services for students with disabilities in postsecondary education settings.

St. Thomas University School of Law (FL), Complaint No. 04-94-2093 (OCR Region IV, 1993).

SUNY Health Science Center at Brooklyn, Complaint No. 02-92-2004, (OCR Region II, 1993).

University of Southern California, Santa Barbara, Complaint No. 09-90-2057 (OCR Region IX, 1993).

United States v. Morant, 843 F. Supp. 1092 (E.D. La 1994).

West, M., Kregel, J., Getzel, E., Zhu, M., Ipsen, S., & Martin, E. (1993). Beyond Section 504: Satisfaction and empowerment of students with disabilities in higher education. *Exceptional Children, 59,* 456–467.

Western State University College of Law, Case No. 09-95-2065-I (OCR Region IX, 1995).

Wynne, v. Tuffs University School of Medicine, 976 F. 2D 791 (1st Cir. 1991).

CHAPTER 6

We tend to treat motivation as if it can be created "by pulling oneself up by one's bootstraps." Instead, motivation follows when areas of strength are fostered, curricula are adapted, potentials are identified, and successes are rewarded.

— Elisabeth Wiig (Gerber & Reiff, 1994)

Student Empowerment

Sally S. Scott

In the previous chapter, we focused on procedural considerations in implementing policy and working with students with disabilities. In this chapter, we will expand on a related program consideration — student empowerment. Unlike procedures for implementing policy, student empowerment is a broad and, in some respects, intangible goal. It involves creating a classroom, program, and campus climate in which students with disabilities have the skills and feel able to advocate for their needs. The presence of student empowerment often distinguishes an OT program that merely meets minimal legal requirements from an OT program that actually achieves an accessible educational environment for student learning and performance.

Student empowerment is not a discrete policy or specific practice. Rather, it is a cumulative process to which faculty can contribute in numerous small and not so small ways. In this chapter, we will provide suggestions for building a climate of student empowerment within the OT program. We provide strategies for individual faculty as well as programmatic supports within the OT department. Finally, we will review research on successful adults with learning disabilities and discuss implications for OT faculty in working with all students with disabilities.

Individual Faculty Strategies

There are a number of faculty actions, strategies, and courtesies that can serve to create an environment of student empowerment for OT students with disabilities. We will examine several strategies for promoting student empowerment, including: reflecting on personal attitudes; advocating for adequate institutional policies and structures; encouraging students to self-identify; and using acceptable terminology and general etiquette.

Reflecting on Personal Attitudes

As a starting point in nurturing an environment of student empowerment, it is important for each individual faculty member to reflect on his or her own behaviors and attitudes toward students with disabilities. As mentioned in chapter 5, one of the most pervasive barriers to access experienced by college students with disabilities is the discriminatory attitudes of faculty, staff, and students on campus (West, Kregel, Getzel, Zhu, Ipsen, & Martin, 1993). Table 6.1 contains a series of questions to foster reflection on your experiences and interactions with students with disabilities. They are intended to prompt your thinking and broaden your awareness of the subtle and overt ways you or other OT faculty may inadvertently be discriminating against OT students with disabilities in the classroom or clinic. The questions may be used on an individual basis as a self-assessment tool, or they may be used as a springboard for discussion in a group activity such as in a faculty inservice, preservice training, departmental discussion, and so forth.

Table 6.1

Self-Assessment of Personal Attitudes Toward Students with Disabilities

(1) When I reflect on an individual student with a disability, what do I see — the limitations and problems or the strengths and the potential?

(2) When I am working with a student with a disability, do I listen to the needs, concerns, and interests of the individual, or do I feel the need to control the situation?

(3) In class, do I involve a student with a disability in activities and discussions to the same extent as other students?

(4) Do I react differently when a student with a disability poses a question or challenges my point of view as compared with when other students challenge or question me?

(5) When I offer assistance to a student with a disability, do I feel okay if the offer is rejected? Do I really trust that the student with a disability can make his or her own decisions?

(6) Do I recognize that angry, quiet, forceful, and withdrawn behaviors are normal for all people, and that these behaviors in and of themselves are nothing to be overly concerned about when displayed by individuals with disabilities?

(7) Do I give my respect, concern, and empathy to the student with a disability, as I would to any student, without becoming overly sympathetic?

(8) Do I feel comfortable that providing reasonable accommodations to students with disabilities serves to provide an equal opportunity rather than an unfair advantage over other students?

Advocating for Adequate Institutional Policies and Structures

One of the most important contributions to student empowerment that individual faculty can provide is the assurance that institutional and OT standards are being maintained and that students with disabilities are receiving the same quality education as all other students. In order to achieve this, OT faculty need to establish proactive policies and procedures for providing access, as discussed at length in the preceding chapters. In addition, however, OT students with disabilities need a broad infrastructure of support on campus. The presence of such structures and practices as comprehensive policies, grievance procedures, and an office for students with disabilities, helps to create a climate in which disability access needs are anticipated as an integral part of campus life. The message is conveyed that:

- The institution is aware of students with disabilities.

- Students are entitled to accommodations (these are not "favors" granted to individual students).

- The institution has considered how to address access needs. Such structures promote student empowerment and are equally valuable to faculty in addressing student access needs and issues. If these structures are not in place on your campus, we recommend that you serve as an advocate and begin the process of discussing and examining how student needs will be addressed on a campuswide basis.

Encouraging Student Self-Identification

In order for students with disabilities to attain the accommodations needed for an equal educational opportunity, they must first self-identify as having a disability and request specific accommodation.

(See chapter 1 for legal requirements and chapter 5 for procedural issues.) Many students with disabilities are often excellent self-advocates and are comfortable discussing accommodation needs with faculty. Other students may not have experience in self-advocating or may feel hesitant to make disability-related needs known. It is in the best interest of both student and faculty for students with disabilities to discuss accommodation needs early in the semester. OT faculty can encourage such disclosure by putting a statement in all course syllabi inviting students to contact the faculty member if disability-related accommodations are needed. For example, a statement such as the following might be used: "If you need accommodation in this class or would like to discuss special learning needs because of a documented disability, please make an appointment during my office hours as early in the semester as possible." As a follow-up, it is also helpful for faculty to make an announcement during the first class session that he or she is available to meet with students to discuss special needs during office hours.

These simple strategies for inviting self-identification serve to increase the comfort of students with disabilities in requesting accommodation and promote an important first step in student empowerment.

Table 6.2
General Principles for Language Usage

1) **Put the person first, not the disability**

examples:		
	• A student with a learning disability	*NOT a learning-disabled student*
	• People with disabilities	*NOT the disabled*

2) **Use appropriate terms**

examples:		
	• Disability	*NOT handicapped, invalid, cripple*
	• Nondisabled	*NOT normal, healthy*
	• Specific disability terms	

3) **State the facts — avoid emotional terms**

examples:		
	• An individual *has* a disability or	*NOT afflicted with, victim of,*
	• An individual *with* a disability	*suffers from, etc.*

4) **State the facts — avoid euphemisms**

examples:		
	• A person with a physical, sensory, or mental disability	*NOT handi-capable, inconvenienced, differently-abled, etc.*

5) **State the facts — be accurate**

examples:		
	• A person uses a wheelchair	*NOT wheelchairbound, confined to a wheelchair, etc.*

Terminology

Language usage is an important factor in conveying attitudes and awareness about disabilities and has the potential to further contribute to or detract from student empowerment (Table 6.2). Over the years, preferred terminology has emerged that is considered appropriate, accurate, and considerate when referring to individuals with disabilities. As with the rest of the English language, appropriate usage and terminology are still evolving. In addition to demonstrating respect for individuals with disabilities, awareness of the issues and principles behind preferred language can serve to increase OT faculty understanding of the many stereotypes and barriers people with disabilities typically face.

Several general principles have evolved defining the conventions of acceptable language usage in the area of disabilities (see Table 6.2). The principles are simple and straightforward and, for the most part, merely entail an awareness of potential issues:

(1) *Put the person first, not the disability.*
Students with disabilities that you work with are more like other students than they are different. It is important to emphasize the individual rather than highlighting a functional limitation.

(2) *Use appropriate terms.*
The term *disability* applies to the functional limitations of an individual. Such terms as multiple sclerosis, epilepsy, attention deficit, paraplegia, or deafness are all forms of disability. The word *handicap* derives from the early word usage of "hand to cap," literally conveying the need for individuals with disabilities to beg for a living by extending their hats for donations. The negative overtones of the term are obvious. The term has now evolved to mean an environmental or attitudinal barrier. For example, a student uses a wheelchair because of a disability. If the student cannot attend class because the class is being held on the second floor of a building with no elevator, the student then is handicapped by the situation. The term *cripple* has a similar negative word lineage, from the Old English *to creep* and is not an acceptable descriptor for disabilities. When talking about people without disabilities, it is appropriate to refer to them as *nondisabled*. Using the terms *normal* or *healthy* in comparison implies that the opposite is true of people with disabilities — that they are not normal or not healthy. When referring to specific disabilities it is important to avoid jargon or colloquial terms (see Table 6.3 for recommended terminology).

Table 6.3
Preferred Terminology in Referring to Individuals with Disabilities

Hearing loss:
- Person who is deaf
- Person who is hard of hearing

Visual impairment:
- Person who is blind
- Person with a visual impairment

Mobility impairment:
- Person who uses a wheelchair
- Wheelchair user
- Person with quadriplegia, cerebral palsy, etc.

Learning disability
- Person with a learning disability

Mental health impairment
- Person who has depression, person with schizophrenia, etc.

(3) *State the facts — avoid emotional terms.*
Stating that a person *has* a disability is an objective statement. In contrast, describing a person as "afflicted with," "stricken by," or "suffering from" a disability adds an emotional overlay that connotes helplessness, dependency, or defeat.

(4) *State the facts — avoid euphemisms.*
Sometimes efforts to emphasize the individuality and abilities of people with disabilities become overzealous. Terms such as *physically challenged, handicapable*, or *differently abled*, though well intentioned, are unnecessary euphemisms that are perceived by some as degrading and avoiding reality.

(5) *State the facts — be accurate.*
People with disabilities use wheelchairs, crutches, or other assistive technology to promote mobility and independence. They are not *wheelchair bound* or *confined to crutches*. They typically regard these aids as liberating. To convey this, terms and phrases such as *wheelchair user* or *walks with crutches* are acceptable.

General Etiquette

In addition to being aware of acceptable language usage, there are some common courtesies for interacting with individuals with disabilities. The first step in interacting with individuals with disabilities is to treat them as you would anybody else. OT students with disabilities come to college for the same reasons other students do. They bring with them the same range of backgrounds, experiences, skills, and abilities. The suggestions in Table 6.4 are based on tips offered by the National Easter Seal Society to guide everyday interactions with individuals with disabilities.

Table 6.4
General Etiquette for Interacting with Individuals with Disabilities

1. When talking with a person who has a disability, look at and speak directly to that person, rather than to a companion, interpreter, or attendant who may be present.

2. Ask before you help. If the offer to help is declined, do not insist. If the offer is accepted, listen to or ask for instructions.

3. Relax. Don't be embarrassed if you happen to use common expressions such as "see you later" or "got to be running along." People with disabilities also use these expressions.

4. When talking with someone in a wheelchair, do not lean on the wheelchair. It is part of the person's body space. Hanging on or leaning on the wheelchair is similar to leaning on a person sitting in a chair.

5. When talking with a person in a wheelchair for more than a few minutes, sit down in order to place yourself at the person's eye level.

6. To get the attention of a person with a hearing loss, tap the person on the shoulder or wave your hand. Look directly at the person and speak clearly. Show consideration by facing a light source and keeping your hands away from your mouth while speaking. Shouting won't help but written notes are fine for short conversations.

7. When greeting someone with a vision impairment, always identify yourself and others who may be with you. Speak in a normal tone of voice, indicate when you move from place to place, and let it be known when the conversation is at an end. If the person needs mobility assistance, allow him or her to take your arm at or above the elbow so that you can guide rather than propel the person.

Note: From the National Easter Seal Society. Reprinted with permission.

Programmatic Supports

In addition to individual faculty awareness and strategies, there are programmatic supports that the OT department may wish to implement to promote student empowerment. Suggestions will be provided for facilitating critical transition periods in the movement from secondary to postsecondary education. OT faculty may wish to develop their own strategies for supporting postsecondary classroom to clinic and postsecondary education to employment transitions.

Support Transitions

As students with and without disabilities cross settings, they experience changes in responsibility and expectations. For example, as students enter college for the first time, there are increased academic demands, greater needs for autonomy and independence, and new expectations in managing the demands of independent living. In recognition of the need for aiding smooth transitions, colleges are increasingly providing support such as freshman year programs to aid retention or various internships to aid graduates in the transition to employment. In addition to the common stresses of transition, the differences are augmented for students with disabilities because change entails the additional considerations of support services and access issues. Students with disabilities are at greater risk of encountering discrimination and barriers as they face critical transition periods moving between environments and/or systems that have different operating practices, different levels of support, or even different legal mandates for access.

Secondary to Postsecondary

As students with disabilities make the transition from high school to college, they experience a change in legal status. Through high school, students with disabilities are provided with specific services for an appropriate and individual education as specified under the Individuals with Disabilities Education Act (IDEA, P.L. 101-476, 1990). When students graduate from high school, the emphasis of the law changes.

Individuals with disabilities are no longer assured of special services, but rather are protected from discrimination on the basis of disability under Section 504 and the ADA.

As a direct result of differing legal mandates, the move from high school to college also entails different levels of support for students with disabilities. In high school, a cascade of services is often available, ranging from self-contained special education classes, to use of a resource room for one or more class periods, to full inclusion in regular classes. In college, special courses are rarely offered, and students attend regular classes with all other students. Emphasis is on providing access to information and learning through accommodations rather than providing remediation or special services.

A third dramatic change in the transition to college is the differing operating practices and responsibilities of support services and students. In high school, the school staff is responsible for seeking out students in need of support, providing diagnostic services, and developing an individual education plan. Parents are legally required and often encouraged to be actively involved in the process. In contrast to high school services, colleges require students with disabilities to self-identify, provide documentation to the institution, and request specific accommodation. Parental involvement is not encouraged. The students, often for the first time, must be strong self-advocates and may choose whether to access services.

What role should the OT program play in addressing transition needs? As part of IDEA, high schools are required to develop transition plans for students with disabilities to help anticipate and plan for students' future needs after high school. A number of model demonstration projects have been developed in recent years to promote the successful transition to college. These projects typically involve encouraging self-advocacy skills, developing study strategies, and taking appropriate college preparatory coursework. Linkages with colleges in this transition period typically involve information sharing with the campus office for students with disabilities.

The role of the postsecondary OT program staff will be minimal at this point. Communication activities will assist students to gather information about the program and make an educated decision about whether OT is a realistic education and career option. The primary role of the OT program is to disseminate information and provide observational opportunities that accurately portray the requirements, rigor, and standards of the individual OT program (see Chapter 5 for strategies for information dissemination.)

Once students arrive on campus, they will continue to adjust to new context demands and requirements. OT faculty need to be aware of transition issues and stresses and understand that students will be arriving on campus with various backgrounds and levels of preparation. OT faculty may need to provide information on support services and resources available on campus and encourage students with disabilities to self-advocate.

Successful Adults with Learning Disabilities

A major goal of college OT programs is to produce competent professionals in occupational therapy who can provide needed services and promote further growth and advances in the profession. In recent years, researchers in learning disabilities have begun to identify the attributes and qualities of successful adults with learning disabilities (Adelman & Vogel, 1990; Gerber & Reiff, 1994; Spekman, Goldberg, & Herman, 1992). Many of these variables have been described as patterns of behavior that can be taught and nurtured to foster employment success (Gerber & Reiff, 1994). As part of student empowerment in achieving the ultimate goal of completing OT training and advancing to successful professional practice, these variables will be presented and the implications for OT faculty will be proposed. Though this research has focused strictly on individuals with learning disabilities, many of the principles and resulting implications may be useful in promoting empowerment for students with a variety of disabilities.

Factors in Success

In studies examining adults with learning disabilities, individuals demonstrated persisting problems into adulthood, including academic difficulties (Buchanan & Wolf, 1986; Frauenheim & Heckerl, 1983; McCue, Shelly, & Goldstein, 1986). Yet despite these chronic problems, individuals with learning disabilities achieve positive adult outcomes in a number of arenas, including employment.

Ginsburg, Gerber, and Reiff (1994) interviewed a sample of highly successful adults with learning disabilities and identified factors contributing to success. The predominant characteristic in successful adults was identified as control over one's life. *Control* was described as consisting of an interaction of "internal decisions" and subsequent "external manifestations" (Table 6.5).

Internal decisions were made up of three components: desire, goal orientation, and reframing. Desire was demonstrated in successful adults as a strong determination to excel and succeed. Goal orientation was evidenced in explicit, achievable aspirations. Success in short-term goals provided positive feedback and

---

Table 6.5
Factors Identified in Successful Adults with Learning Disabilities

Internal decisions:

- Desire to achieve

- Goal orientation

- Reframing of the disability

External manifestations:

- Persistence of effort

- Goodness of fit with the chosen environment

- Learned creativity in approaching tasks

- Use of a social ecology for support

greater focus in achieving long-term goals. The final component in internal decisions was reframing. Reframing was identified as the process of reinterpreting the learning disability from something dysfunctional to something functional and typically entailed:

- Recognizing the disability
- Accepting the disability
- Understanding the disability
- Taking action to work in areas of individual strength (see Gerber, Reiff, & Ginsberg, 1996, for an in-depth discussion).

These "internal decisions" were then translated into "external manifestations" described as persistence, goodness of fit, learned creativity, and social ecology. Persistence was evidenced in not only the desire to succeed but also the willingness to work hard and persevere toward goals. Goodness of fit involved finding surroundings and environments in which strengths and abilities could be optimized and weaknesses minimized. The process of learned creativity entailed exploring and developing a range of strategies, techniques, devices, or other mechanisms to enhance performance. Successful adults often came up with unique and personal ways to accomplish tasks. And finally, social ecology described the willingness to use a social support system in achieving goals. Successful adults built a network of supporters such as mentors, friends, or a spouse. They avoided dependence and achieved a successful balance between support and autonomy. Ginsberg, Gerber, and Reiff (1994) noted, in conclusion, that "the most striking finding of our research was how well persons who are labeled as learning disabled are able to learn and ultimately succeed." Of particular relevance for OT faculty, the researchers recommended that "each of the internal decisions and external manifestations discovered are variables susceptible to training."

Implications for OT Faculty

The factors of adult success identified by Ginsberg, Gerber, and Reiff (1994) are important variables of which to be aware, but they are certainly not prescriptive findings guaranteeing future student success. They do, however, suggest areas that may be beneficial for student development and support. In Table 6.6, we consider the implications of the research on successful adults with learning disabilities and provide recommended strategies for OT faculty in promoting student success and empowerment. OT faculty will likely find that though these suggestions are particularly important for students with disabilities, many of these recommendations will benefit students without disabilities as well.

The important qualities of desire and persistence are perhaps best taught through modeling and encouragement. Though not necessarily a formal process, OT faculty might look for opportunities to *serve as a mentor or role model* in fostering these qualities in students with disabilities. OT faculty should also encourage student participation in a more formalized OT mentoring program.

Encouraging students to adapt goal orientation in their professional studies is, to some extent, already built into most college programs. Students must clear

---

Table 6.6
Recommendations for OT Faculty in Promoting Factors of Success

- Serve as a mentor or role model

- Provide careful advising to set short-term and long-term goals

- Provide careful advising to identify and work in the areas of student strengths

- Nurture and encourage student creativity

- Encourage appropriate use of institutional support

- Foster development of social ecology

the successive hurdles of college admissions, program prerequisites, classroom requirements, clinical experiences, and so forth. In addition to these broad programmatic goals, however, OT faculty are encouraged to *provide careful advising to set short-term and long-term goals*. Successful adults with learning disabilities noted the importance of building a sense of accomplishmentthrough achieving and celebrating small victories in the process of attaining long-term goals. OT faculty could promote and model goal setting in the classroom (e.g., proving intermediary steps in long-range assignments) or on an individual basis in advising and working with students.

An integral part of goal setting is to encourage the reframing of the disability by focusing on individual student strengths and potential while accomplishing goals for learning and professional growth. OT faculty should provide *careful advising to identify and work in areas of student strength* within the field of OT to promote "goodness of fit" in future professional work environments.

Successful adults demonstrated learned creativity in response to the demands of their professional fields of employment. OT faculty should *nurture and encourage such student creativity* in individual courses and across program requirements whenever possible and appropriate. Some famous innovative thinkers have been identified as having learning disabilities (e.g., Albert Einstein) and have provided valuable contributions to their respective fields because of their divergent ways of approaching tasks.

Upon entering college, some students with disabilities want to shed their disability label and be like other students without disabilities. Though perhaps understandable, these students often experience unnecessary failure (see previous discussion on transition issues, this chapter). Successful adults with learning disabilities use support systems appropriately as a tool for achieving goals. OT faculty should *encourage appropriate use of institutional support*. OT faculty may also look for means to foster *development of a social ecology* or a support network among students through such means as encouraging study groups or assigning collaborative projects and tasks.

Summary

In reading these recommendations, you may find that you are already doing some things to promote the development of these success factors in your students. If so, we hope your awareness of the correlation of these variables with adult success for individuals with learning disabilities will serve to broaden and renew your appreciation of why these activities are important. In addition to considering these recommendations, we urge you to examine these research findings and devise your own strategies for student empowerment as well as inform students of these variables and encourage them to develop their own strategies.

• • •

References

Adelman, P., & Vogel, S. (1990). College graduates with learning disabilities — Employment attainment and career patterns. *Learning Disability Quarterly, 13*, 154–166.

Buchanan, M., & Wolf, J. (1986). A comprehensive study of learning disabled adults. *Journal of Learning Disabilities, 19*, 34–38.

Frauenheim, J., & Heckerl, J. (1983). Longitudinal study of psychological achievement test performance in severe dyslexic adults. *Journal of Learning Disabilities, 16*, 339–347.

Gerber, P., & Reiff, H. (1994). *Learning disabilities in adulthood: Persisting problems and evolving issues.* Boston, MA: Andover Medical Publishers.

Gerber, P., Reiff, H., & Ginsberg, R. (1996). Reframing the learning disabilities experience. *Journal of Learning Disabilities, 29*, 98–101.

Ginsberg, R., Gerber, P., & Reiff, H. (1994). Employment success for adults with learning disabilities. In P. Gerber & H. Reiff (Eds.), *Learning disabilities in adulthood: Persisting problems and evolving issues.* Boston, MA: Andover Medical Publishers.

McCue, M., Shelly, C., & Goldstein, G. (1986). Intellectual, academic, and neuropsychological performance levels in learning disabled adults. *Journal of Learning Disabilities, 19*, 223–236.

Spekman, N., Goldberg, R., & Herman, K. (1992). Learning disabled children grow up: A search for factors related to success in the young adult years. *Learning Disabilities Research & Practice, 7*, 161–170.

West, M., Kregel, J., Getzel, E., Zhu, M., Ipsen, S., & Martin, E. (1993). Beyond Section 504: Satisfaction and empowerment of students with disabilities in higher education. *Exceptional Children, 59*, 456–467.

Recommended Readings

Brinckerhoff, L. (1994). Developing effective self-advocacy skills in college-bound students with learning disabilities. *Intervention in School and Clinic, 29*, 229–237.

Michaels, C. (1994). *Transition strategies for persons with learning disabilities.* San Diego, CA: Singular Publishing Group.

CHAPTER 7

Resources

The advent of the information era has led to the availability of a wealth of information on services to students with disabilities. Resources are available within all ranges of cost, depth, and accessibility. Gathering resources is usually both an ongoing and immediate process that is undertaken by both the educator and the student. The resource list presented here is, of necessity, selective but should serve as a starting point for gathering information and pursuing other resources.

On-Campus Resources

- Americans with Disabilities Coordinator
- 504 Campus Coordinator
- Disabled Student Services
- Learning Resource Center or Program
- Campus Library and Literature Search
- Internet

Local Resources—State

The key to obtaining pertinent data from local resources (see the list, below) is to request information about adults who are enrolled in postsecondary education and who have a specific disability. Resources often focus on a person's age, employment, or education status, and the nature of the disability. Be sure to clarify with each student what his or her specific needs are.

- Local Support Groups for a Specific Disability
- Local Support Groups for Adult Literacy
- Local Support Groups for Employment
- State Offices of Vocational Rehabilitation, Higher Education, and Health

Regional Resources— Office of Civil Rights

The Office of Civil Rights (OCR), United States Department of Education, maintains regional offices to answer questions related to Section 504 of the Rehabilitation Act of 1973. The regional offices for education can provide information on education and Section 504. The offices for health and human services can provide information on the impact of Section 504 on health fields.

Government Offices — Section 504

U.S. Department of Justice
Stewart Oneglia
Coordination and Review Section
PO Box 66118
Washington, DC 20035-6118
202 307-2222
202 514-0301 (ADA hotline)
L. Irene Bowen Civil Rights Division

U.S. Department of Education
Office for Civil Rights
Room 5000
330 C St., SW
Washington, DC 20202-1100
202 205-5413
202 205-9683 (TDD)

REGION I (Connecticut, Maine, Massachusetts, New Hampshire, Rhode Island, Vermont)

U.S. Department of Education
J.W. McCormack Post Office and Courthouse
Room 222
Boston, MA 02109-4557
617 223-9667
617 223-9695 (TDD)

REGION II (New Jersey, New York, Puerto Rico, Virgin Islands)

U.S. Department of Education
26 Federal Plaza, Room 33-130
New York, NY 10278
212 264-4633
212 264-9464 (TDD)

REGION III (Delaware, District of Columbia, Maryland, Pennsylvania, Virginia, West Virginia)

U.S. Department of Education
3535 Market St.
Room 6300
Philadelphia, PA 19104-3326
215 596-6787
215 596-6794 (TDD)

REGION IV (Alabama, Florida, Georgia, Kentucky, Mississippi, North Carolina, South Carolina, Tennessee)

U.S. Department of Education
101 Marietta Tower Building, Suite 2702
PO Box 2048
Atlanta, GA 30301
404 331-2954
404 331-7236 (TDD)

REGION V (Illinois, Indiana, Michigan, Minnesota, Ohio, Wisconsin)

U.S. Department of Education
401 S. State St., Seventh Floor
Chicago, IL 60605
312 353-2520
312 353-2540 (TDD)

REGION VI (Arkansas, Louisiana, New Mexico, Oklahoma, Texas)

U.S. Department of Education
1200 Main Tower Building, Suite 2260
Dallas, TX 75202
214 767-3959
214 767-3639 (TDD)

REGION VII (Iowa, Kansas, Missouri, Nebraska)

U.S. Department of Education
10220 N. Executive Hills Blvd. , Eighth Floor
Kansas City, MO 64153-1367
816 891-8026
816 374-6461 (TDD)

REGION VIII (Colorado, Montana, North Dakota, South Dakota, Utah, Wyoming)

U.S. Department of Education
1244 Speer Blvd., Suite 310
Denver, CO 80204-3582
303 844-5695
303 844-3417 (TDD)

REGION IX (Arizona, California, Hawaii, Nevada, Guam, American Samoa, Northern Mariana Islands, Trust Territory of the Pacific Islands)

U.S. Department of Education
50 United Nations Plaza, Room 239
San Francisco, CA 94102
415 556-7000
415 556-6806 (TDD)

REGION X (Alaska, Idaho, Oregon, Washington)

U.S. Department of Education
Henry Jackson Federal Building
Mail Code 10-9010
915 Second Ave., Room 3310
Seattle, WA 98174-1099
206 553-6811
206 553-6419 (TDD)

Office of Civil Rights

U.S. Department of Health and Human Services
Office for Civil Rights
Edward Mercado, Director
Cohen Building
330 Independence Ave., SW, Room 5400
Washington, DC 20201
202 619-0403
202 472-2916 (TDD)

REGION I (Connecticut, Maine, Massachusetts, New Hampshire, Rhode Island, Vermont)

U.S. Department of Health and Human Services
John F. Kennedy Federal Building, Room 1875
Government Center
Boston, MA 02203
617 565-1340
617 565-2355 (TDD)

REGION II (New Jersey, New York, Puerto Rico, Virgin Islands)

U.S. Department of Health and Human Services
26 Federal Plaza
Room 3312
New York, NY 10278
212 264-3313
212 264-2355 (TDD)

REGION III (Delaware, District of Columbia, Maryland, Pennsylvania, Virginia, West Virginia)

U.S. Department of Health and Human Services
Gateway Building, 3535 Market St., Room 6350
PO Box 13716
215 596-1262
215 596-5195 (TDD)

REGION IV (Alabama, Florida, Georgia, Kentucky, Mississippi, North Carolina, South Carolina, Tennessee)

U.S. Department of Health and Human Services
101 Marietta Tower Building, Suite 1502
Atlanta, GA 30323
404 331-2779
404 331-2867 (TDD)

REGION V (Illinois, Indiana, Michigan, Minnesota, Ohio, Wisconsin)

U.S. Department of Health and Human Services
105 W. Adams St.
Chicago, IL 60603
312 886-2359
312 353-5693 (TDD)

REGION VI (Arkansas, Louisiana, New Mexico, Oklahoma, Texas)

U.S. Department of Health and Human Services
1200 Main Tower Building
Suite 1360
Dallas, TX 75202
214 767-4056
214-767-8940 (TDD)

REGION VII (Iowa, Kansas, Missouri, Nebraska)

U.S. Department of Health and Human Services
601 W. 12th
Room 248
Kansas City, MO 64106
816 426-7277
816 426-7065 (TDD)

REGION VIII (Colorado, Montana, North Dakota, South Dakota, Utah, Wyoming)

U.S. Department of Health and Human Services
Federal Office Building
1961 Stout St.
Room 844
Denver, CO 80294
303 844-2024
303 844-8439 (TDD)

REGION IX (Arizona, California, Hawaii, Nevada, Guam, American Samoa, Northern Mariana Islands, Trust Territory of the Pacific Islands)

U.S. Department of Health and Human Services
50 UN Plaza, Room 322
San Francisco, CA 94102
415 556-8586 (Voice TDD)

REGION X (Alaska, Idaho, Oregon, Washington)

U.S. Department of Health and Human Services
2201 Sixth Ave.
Mail Stop XII
Seattle, WA 98121
206 553-0473
206 553-7486 (TDD)

Regional Disability and Business Technical Assistance Centers (DBTACs) — Contact for Information on the ADA

REGION I (Connecticut, Maine, Massachusetts, New Hampshire, Rhode Island, Vermont)

New England DBTAC
145 Newbury St.
Portland, ME 04101
207 874-6535 (Voice/TDD)

REGION II (New Jersey, New York, Puerto Rico, Virgin Islands)

Northeast DBTAC
United Cerebral Palsy Association of New Jersey
354 South Broad St.
Trenton, NH 08608
609 392-4004 (Voice)
609 392-7004 (TDD)

REGION III (Delaware, District of Columbia, Maryland, Pennsylvania, Virginia, West Virginia)

Mid Atlantic DBTAC
Independence Center of Northern Virginia
2111 Wilson Blvd.
Suite 400
Arlington, VA 22201
703 525-3268 (Voice/TDD)

REGION IV (Alabama, Florida, Georgia, Kentucky, Mississippi, North Carolina, South Carolina, Tennessee)

Southeast DBTAC
United Cerebral Palsy Association, Inc./
National Alliance of Business
1776 Peachtree St.
Suite 310 North
Atlanta, GA 30309
404 888-0022 (Voice)
404 888-9098 (TDD)

REGION V (Illinois, Indiana, Michigan, Minnesota, Ohio, Wisconsin)

Great Lakes DBTAC
University of Illinois at Chicago/UAP
1640 West Roosevelt Rd. M/C 627
Chicago, IL 60608
312 413-7756 (Voice/TDD)

REGION VI (Arkansas, Louisiana, New Mexico, Oklahoma, Texas)

Southwest DBTAC
Independent Living Research Utilization/
The Institute for Rehabilitation and Research
2323 South Sheperd St., Suite 1000
Houston, TX 77019
713 520-0232 (Voice)
713 520-5136 (TDD)

REGION VII (Iowa, Kansas, Missouri, Nebraska)

Great Plains DBTAC
University of Missouri at Columbia
4816 Santana Dr.
Columbia, MO 65203
314 882-3600 (Voice/TDD)

REGION VIII (Colorado, Montana, North Dakota, South Dakota, Utah, Wyoming)

Rocky Mountain DBTAC
Meeting the Challenge, Inc.
3630 Sinton Rd.
Suite 103
Colorado Springs, CO 80907-5072
719 444-0252 (Voice/TDD)

REGION IX (Arizona, California, Hawaii, Nevada, Pacific Basin)

Pacific DBTAC
Berkeley Planning Associates
440 Grand Ave., Suite 500
Oakland, CA 94610
510 465-7884 (Voice)
510 465-3172 (TDD)

REGION X (Alaska, Idaho, Oregon, Washington)

Northwest DBTAC
Washington State Governor's Committee
PO Box 9046
Olympia, WA 98507-9046
206 438-3168 (Voice)
206 438-3167 (TDD)

Other Government Resources

Access Board
1331 F St., NW, Suite 1000
Washington, DC 20004-1111
202 272-5434 (general information)
202 272-5449 (TDD)
800 USA-ABLE (ADA hotline)

Department of Education Clearinghouse on
Disability Information
330 C St., SW, Room 3132
Washington, DC 20202-2524
202 205-8723 (Voice/TDD)

Department of Education Rehabilitation Services
Administration
330 C St., SW, Room 3028
Washington, DC 20202
202 205-5482
202 205-8848 (TDD)

*Programs of the Rehabilitation Services Administration
deal with the supervision, management, development,
and promotion of the provisions of the Rehabilitation
Act of 1973, exclusive of Sections 502, 503, and 504.*

Department of Education Special Education
Programs
330 C St., SW, Room 3086
Washington, DC 20202
202 205-5507
202 205-9754 (TDD)
National Council on Disability
800 Independence Ave., SW, Suite 814
Washington, DC 20591
202 267-3235
202 267-3232 (TDD)

National Institute on Disability and Rehabilitation
Research
400 Maryland Ave., SW
Washington, DC 20202-2572

National Library Services for the Blind and
Physically Handicapped
1291 Taylor St., NW
Washington, DC 20542
202 707-5100
202 707-0778 (TDD)

President's Committee on Employment of People
with Disabilities
1331 F St., NW Suite 300
Washington, DC 20004
202 376-6200
202 376-6205 (TDD)

U.S. Congress Subcommittee on Disability Policy
(Senate Committee on Labor and Human
Resources)
Hart Senate Office Building, Room 113
Washington, DC 20510
202 224-6265
202 224-3457 (TDD)

U.S. Congress Subcommittee on Select Education
(House Committee on Education and Labor)
518 O'Neill House Office Building
Washington, DC 20515
202 226-7532 (Voice/TDD)

National Resources

National advocacy, professional, and student resources can provide detailed information on their specialty area as well as contacts for local resources on the
same specialty. Information requests should be as specific as possible, clarifying the student's disability, program of study, and questions needed to be answered.

The Association for Persons with Severe
Handicaps
11202 Greenwood Avenue
Seattle, WA 98133
206 361-8870

Association on Higher Education and Disability
(AHEAD)
PO Box 21192
Columbus, OH 43221
614 488-4972

A professional organization for educators committed to promoting full participation of individuals with disabilities in college. The organization maintains a large number of publications regarding postsecondary education for persons with disabilities.

Center on Education and Work
University of Wisconsin
964 Educational Sciences Building
1025 West Johnson St.
Madison, WI 53706-1796
800 466-0399

Conducts research and disseminated information concerning work issues and disability. Many resources are available for students, instructors, and administrators.

Children with Attention Deficit Disorders
(CHADD)
499 Northwest 70th Ave., Suite 308
Plantation, FL 33317
305 587-3700

Provides information on attention deficit disorders.

Epilepsy Foundation of America
4351 Garden City Dr.
Landover, MD 20785-2267
301 459-3700
800 EFA-4050

Provides programs and services for individuals with epilepsy (seizure disorders) and their families, including a comprehensive library that focuses on epilepsy issues.

ERIC Clearinghouse on Adult. Career, and
Vocational Education
The Ohio State University
1960 Kenny Rd.
Columbus, OH 43210
614 486-3655

Identifies, selects, processes, and disseminates information on education. Services include: microfiche or paper copies of materials, review and synthesis of papers, and computer searches.

Publications:
The ABLE Sampler: A Professional Development
Guide for Adult Literacy
Practitioners Teaching Adults with Learning
Disabilities (ERIC Digest No. 99)
Adult Literacy
Learner Assessment (ERIC Digest No. 103)
A Special Project for the Development of
Assessment and Educational Programming
Techniques for Serving the Adult Basic Education
Student with Learning Disabilities; Adult
Learning Problems
Insights Instruction, Implications
Academic Assessment and Remediation of Adults
with Learning Disabilities: A Resource Series for
Adult Education Teachers.

Health Resource Center
One Dupont Circle, Suite 800
Washington, DC 20036-1193
800 544-3284

Provides information on postsecondary education for individuals with disabilities. Publications: Community Colleges and Students with Disabilities: A Directory of Services and Programs; Distance Learning; HEALTH Resource Directory; Resources for Adults with Learning Disabilities; and a variety of fact sheets on postsecondary education for persons with disabilities.

Job Accommodations Network (JAN)
President's Committee on Employment of People
with Disabilities
West Virginia University
809 Allen Hall
PO Box 6213
Morgantown, WV 26506-6123
800 526-7234
304 293-7186

Learning Disabilities Association of America
4156 Library Rd.
Pittsburgh, PA 15234
412 341-1515
412 341-8077

A national organization devoted to defining and finding solutions for the broad spectrum of learning disabilities. A wide variety of books, pamphlets, and publications is available. Publication: A Learning Disabilities Digest for Literacy Providers.

Learning Resources Network (LERN)
1554 Hayes
Manhattan, KS 66502
913 539-5376

Provides resources for adult education and adult basic education service providers. Publication: Programming Resource Guide.

Mainstream
3 Bethesda Metro Center, Suite 830
Bethesda, MD 20814
301 654-2400

Contact Mainstream for a host of employment-related services including publications, technical assistance, and job referral services (Project Link).

National Brain Injury Foundation
1140 Connecticut Avenue, NW, Suite 812
Washington, DC 20036
202 296-6443

Offers services to survivors, families, professionals/ service providers, including the following: a helpline; referral sources; educational symposia to rehabilitation personnel and attorneys; and various publications (e.g., The Educator's Manual).

National Information Center for Children and
Youth with Disabilities
PO Box 1492
Washington, DC 20013-1492
800 999-5599

Provides information to assist parents, educators, caregivers, and advocates in helping children and youth with disabilities become participating members of the community. Publications: News Digest and Summary and Reading and Learning Disabilities: A Resource Guide.

National Information Center on Deafness
(NICD)–HI
Gallaudet University
MLC-LE50
800 Florida Ave., NE
Washington, DC 20002
202 651-5051 (Voice)
202 651-5052 (TTD)

Serves as a centralized source of information on topics dealing with deafness and hearing loss including education of deaf children, communication, hearing loss and aging, careers in deafness, and assistive devices. Each request for information is answered through selected materials, personalized letters, and/or referrals to experts and supporting agencies.

National Rehabilitation Information Center
8455 Colesville Rd., Suite 935
Silver Spring, MD 20910-3319
800 346-2742

Provides disability and rehabilitation research and resources, including commercially published books, journal articles, and audiovisual materials.

National Spinal Cord Injury Association
600 W. Cummings Park, Suite 2000
Woburn, MA 01801
617 935-2722
800 962-9629
800 638-1733 in Maryland

Orton Dyslexia Society
742 York Rd.
Towson, MD 21204
800 222-3123

Provides information on dyslexia, hosts national and local conferences, and publishes a professional journal: Annals of Dyslexia.

New England Branch Office
Linden Hill School
South Mountain Rd.
Northfield, MA 01360
413 498-2906

*Provides resources and referrals to educational special-
ists as well as other resource information.*

Paralyzed Veterans of America
801 11th St., NW
Washington, DC 20006
202 872-1300

President's Committee on Employment of People
with Disabilities
1111 20th St., NW, Suite 636
Washington, DC 20036-5050
202 653-5044

*Seeks to increase employment among all people with dis-
abilities through conferences, publications, and policy development.*

The Rebus Institute
198 Taylor Blvd., Suite 201
Millbrae, CA 94030
415 697-7424

*A nonprofit research institute devoted to the study and
dissemination of information related to adults with learning differences.*

Recording for the Blind
The Anne T. MacDonald Center
20 Roszel Rd.
Princeton, NJ 08540
800 221-4792
609 452-0606

*Provides educational and professional books in acces-
sible media format to people with print disabilities. RFB
has an extensive free library of books on audiocassette, covering a wide range of subjects and academic levels. Services
are available to persons with a verified visual, physical, or
specific learning disability that substantially limits reading. Also, taped educational materials are available free*

*for blind and disabled students. Currently, there are some
42,000 titles available at 20 centers around the country.*

Registry of Interpreters for the Deaf, Inc.
8719 Colesville Rd., Suite 310
Silver Spring, MD 20910
301 608-0050 (Voice/TDD)

Resource Center on Substance Abuse Prevention
and Disability
VA Educational Services
1331 F St., NW, Suite 800
Washington, DC 20004
202 783-2900

*Provides up-to-date information about programs, re-
sources, reference materials, and research in the areas of substance abuse and disability issues. Publications: Drug
Abuse Prevention for People with Disabilities; Resource Center News.*

Rochester Institute of Technology
National Technical Institute for the Deaf
Public Information Office
Johnson Building, PO Box 9887
Rochester, NY 14623-0887
716 475-6824 (Voice)
716 475-2181 (TDD)

Telecommunications for the Deaf, Inc.
8719 Colesville Rd., Suite 310
Silver Spring, MD 20910
301 589-3043 (Voice/TDD)

*Consulting agency providing information and assistance
on telecommunication issues. Also publishes a directory of
TDD numbers.*

United Cerebral Palsy Association
1522 K St., Suite 1112
Washington, DC 20005
202 842-1266

World Institute on Disability
510 16th St., Suite 100
Oakland, CA 94612
415 763-4100

Publications

Accent on Living: Buyer's Guide
PO Box 700
Bloomington, IL 61702
309 378-2961

Access Board
1111 18th St., NW, Suite 501
Washington, DC 20036
202 653-7834
Distributes several free publications.

Access to the Past
American Association for State and Local History
530 Church St., Suite 600
Nashville, TN 32719
615 255-2971

This book gives guidance on renovating historic facilities to make them accessible.

Adult Basic Education and General Educational Development Programs for Disabled Adults: A Handbook for Literacy Tutors and Instructors
Library for the Blind and Physically Handicapped
Free Library of Philadelphia
919 Walnut St.
Philadelphia, PA 19107

The Complete Directory for People with Disabilities
Grey House Publishing
Pocket Knife Square
PO Box 1866
Lakeville, CT 06039

Directory of Human Resources to Better Serve Learners with Special Needs in Vocational Education
National Center for Research in Vocational Education
Materials Distribution Service
Western Illinois University
46 Horrabin Hall
Macomb, IL 61455
800 637-7652

Directory of National Information Sources on Handicapping Conditions and Related Services
U.S. Department of Education
Clearinghouse on Disability Information
Washington, DC 20202
202 205-8241
Free

Guide to U.S. Department of Education Programs
U.S. Department of Education
Washington, DC 20202
202 205-8241
Free

In the Mainstream
Fritz Rumpel, Editor
Mainstream
3 Bethesda Metro Center, Suite 830
Bethesda, MD 20814
301 654-2400

Mental Disability Law Reporter
American Bar Association
Commission on the Mentally Disabled
1800 M St., NW, South Lobby
Washington, DC 20036
202 331-2200

OSERS News in Print
U.S. Department of Education
Clearinghouse on Disability Information
Washington, DC 20202
202 205-8241
Free

Peer Mentoring: A Support Group Model for Students with Learning Disabilities
AHEAD
PO Box 21192
Columbus, OH 43221-0192
614 488-4972

Pocket Guide to Federal Help for Individuals with Disabilities
U.S. Department of Education
Clearinghouse on Disability Information
Washington, DC 20202
202 205-8241
Free

Report on Disability Programs
Business Publishers, Inc.
951 Pershing Drive
Silver Spring, MD 20910
301 587-6300

Resources for Learning Disabilities in Adults
The Adult Training and Development Network of
Connecticut
One Barnard Ln.
Bloomfield, CT 06002
203 242-8883

Working with Adults Who Have Learning
Disabilities (by N. Gregory and P. Weyerts)
Manhattan Adult Learning and Resource Center
2031 Casement Rd.
Manhattan, KS 66502

Technology

Apple Computer, Inc.
National Special Education Alliance
Worldwide Disability Solutions Group
20525 Mariani Ave., 36 SE
Cupertino, CA 95014
408 974-7910

These are two of Apple's projects providing information and technical assistance about Apple computer technologies appropriate to meet the special education and rehabilitation needs of people with a wide range of disabilities.

Center for Special Education Technology
The Council for Exceptional Children
1920 Association Dr.
Reston, VA 22091
703 620-3660
800 873-8255

The Center is a national resource for information about the use of technology in the education of students with disabilities. Information services emphasize trends and practices in technology use as well as resources available to technology users.

Center for Applied Special Technology (CAST)
39 Cross St.
Peabody, MA 01960
508 531-8555 (Voice)

CAST was founded in 1984 to expand opportunities for individuals with special needs through innovative use of computers and related technology. It works with children and adults whose disabilities interfere with the full expression of their capacities for education, employment, or development. Assessment and training services are offered for individuals with a wide range of special needs.

Closing the Gap (CTG)
PO Box 68
Henderson, MN 56044
612 248-3294

CTG published a bimonthly newspaper on microcomputer applications for disabled individuals with an emphasis on special education and rehabilitation uses ($26.00/year).

Computer Able Network
PO Box 1706
Portland, OR 97207
503 645-0009

The Network provides evaluations, training, adaptive computer systems, and assistance in Section 504 compliance. They determine viable, cost-effective solutions for persons of any ability level through adaptive technology and training. The Network offers a unique videotape training program in adaptive computer technology.

IBM National Support Center for Persons with
Disabilities
4111 Northside Parkway
Atlanta, GA 30327
800 426-2133
800 284-9482 (TDD)

The Center responds to requests for information on how computers can help people with a wide range of disabilities to use personal computers. While the Center is unable to diagnose or prescribe an assistive device of software, free information is provided on what is available and where one can go for more details.

Index

A

Academic adjustment, 4, 39
Academic requirements, waiving, 41
Admissions
    Americans with Disabilities Act, 1
    essential program requirements, 53—55
    occupational therapy standards and policies, 53—55
    Section 504, 2
    standards, 17—18
Adult with learning disabilities, 75—76
    occupational therapy faculty, 76
    success factors, 75
Alternative testing procedures, 39, 40
Americans with Disabilities Act
    academic adjustments, 4
    academic and technical admission standards, 3—4
    admission, 3
    applicability, 1
    auxiliary aid, 4
    compliance officer, 12
    definition of disability, 16
        exclusions, 16
    employment assistance, 5
    faculty rights and responsibilities, 5—7
    financial assistance, 5
    housing, 5
    integration process, 47—48
    reasonable accommodation, 5—7
    recruitment, 3
    student rights and responsibilities, 5—7
    terminology, 2
    Title II, 15, 16
        categories of individuals with disabilities, 16
    treatment of students, 3—4
Auxiliary aid, 41, 4
    Americans with Disabilities Act, 4
    Section 104, 4

C

College access
    campus support structures, 9—10
    campus-wide disability advisory board, 13
    existing structures, 9
    faculty with relevant expertise, 13
    linkages, 11, 12, 74
    required campus access services, 9
    resources, 11, 12
    support office philosophy, 10
Communication, honoring communication choice, 41
Compliance officer
    Americans with Disabilities Act, 12
    Section 504, 12
Computer equipment, 43—44
Confidentiality, 46
Contractual agreement, 44—46
    disability disclosure, 46

D

Disability Advisory Board, 13

Disability and Business Technical Assistance Centers, 82—83

Disability documentation, 5

Documentation, 33—34

    dissemination, 34

E

Education for disabled persons

    legal foundation, 1—7

    right to, 15

Educational materials, alternative formats, 43

Employment assistance

    Americans with Disabilities Act, 5

    Section 104, 5

Equal access

    faculty responsibilities, 60—61

    programmatic supports, 74

    student responsibilities, 72

    transitions, 74—75

Essential program requirements, 25—33

    admissions, 55—57

    College of St. Scholastica, Occupational Therapy Department, Contract of Professional Behaviors, 31—32

    defined, 25

    determining clinical and fieldwork requirements, 29

    determining essential components, 26—28

    dissemination, 53—55

    establishment, 26

    faculty outreach, 54

    identifying, 26

    Lasell College Occupational Therapy Assistant Program, 33

    Lourdes College Occupational Therapy Assistant Program, 23—25

    occupational therapy program accessibility, 57

    program minimum skills, 19—20

    recruitment, 55—57

    samples, 19—25, 29—33

    student education outreach, 54

    Texas Women's University, 29—31

University of Minnesota Occupational Therapy Student Performance Essentials and Critical Demands, 21—23

University of Minnesota Programs in Occupational and Physical Therapy: Clinical/Fieldwork Environment Checklist, 20—21

uses, 55

writing, 28

F

Faculty

    advocating for institutional policies and structures, 69

    encouraging student self-identification, 70—71

    personal attitudes, 69

    rights and responsibilities

        Americans with Disabilities Act, 5—7

        Section 504, 5—7

Fee for services, 41—42

Fieldwork, 44—46, 65—67

    clinical site accessibility, 65

    coordination, 65

    disability disclosure, 46

    frequent questions, 65—67

Financial assistance

    Americans with Disabilities Act, 5

    Section 104, 5

G

Government resources, 79—83

H

Housing

    Americans with Disabilities Act, 5

    Section 504, 5

I

Interpreter services, 42

L

Language usage, 71, 72—73

N

National resources, 83—86
Notetakers, 42

O

Occupational therapy standards and policies
    admissions, 55—57
    dissemination, 53—54
    faculty outreach, 54
    occupational therapy program accessibility, 57
    recruitment, 55—57
    student education outreach, 54
    uses, 55
Office for Students with Disabilities, 10—11
    benefits, 12
        campuses lacking, 11
        diagnostic testing, 10
        documentation, 10—11
        faculty resources, 13
        functions, 10—11
        location, 10
        occupational therapy students with disabilities, 12
        personnel, 10
    Office of Civil Rights, 79—81
    On-campus resources, 79

P

Personal attendants, 44
Personal services, 44
Printed materials, 43
Public education, 15
Publications, 87—88

Q

Qualified reader, 43
Qualified student, defined, 15—16

R

Readers, 43
Real-time stenocaptioning, 42
Reasonable accommodations
    Americans with Disabilities Act, 1—7
    defined, 37—38
    denial, 61—64
    dissatisfaction with, 44
    faculty responsibilities, 59—60
    legitimate objections, 64—65
    process, 46—48
    request processing, 59—60
    Section 104, 5—7
    student responsibilities, 59—60
    teaching methods, 62—63
Recruitment
    Americans with Disabilities Act, 3
    essential program requirements, 53—55
    occupational therapy standards and policies, 53—55
    Section 104, 3
Rehabilitation Act of 1973. *See Section 504*
Resources, 79—88

S

Section 504, 1—2, 45
    academic adjustments, 4
    academic and technical admission standards, 3—4
    accessible areas, 3—4
    admission, 3
    auxiliary aid, 4
    compliance officer, 12
    employment assistance, 5
    faculty rights and responsibilities, 5—7
    financial assistance, 5
    government offices, 79—80

housing, 5
implementing regulations, 2 — 3
integration process, 47 — 48
reasonable accommodation, 5 — 7
recruitment, 3
student rights and responsibilities, 5 — 7
terminology, 2
treatment of students, 3 — 4
Speakers' bureau, 13
State resources, 79
Stenocaptioning, 42
Student advocacy group, 13
Student empowerment, 69 — 77
faculty strategies, 68 — 73
Student with disabilities
etiquette, 71
legal foundation, 1 — 7
rights and responsibilities
Americans with Disabilities Act, 5 — 7
Section 104, 5 — 7
students who self-identify, 57 — 58
students with suspected disabilities, 58 — 59
terminology, 71, 72 — 73
working with individual students, 57 — 65

Tape recorder, 41
Taped texts, 43
Technical standards, 17 — 25
academic readiness, 18
criteria, 17 — 18
defined, 17
determination of, 18 — 19
developing, 18 — 19
essential eligibility requirements, 17
essential function of program, 18
Lourdes College Occupational Therapy Assistant Program, 23 — 25
necessary or essential eligibility standards, 19
program minimum skills, 19 — 20
samples, 19 — 25
University of Minnesota Occupational Therapy Student Performance Essentials and Critical Demands, 21 — 23
University of Minnesota Programs in Occupational and Physical Therapy: Clinical/Fieldwork Environment Checklist, 20 — 21
Technology resources, 88
Test administration, 18 — 19
accommodations, 39, 40
additional time, 39, 41
Transition, 74 — 75